George Smith

The Cassiterides

An inquiry into the commercial operations of the Phoenicians in Western Europe

George Smith

The Cassiterides

An inquiry into the commercial operations of the Phoenicians in Western Europe

ISBN/EAN: 9783742840073

Manufactured in Europe, USA, Canada, Australia, Japa

Cover: Foto ©Andreas Hilbeck / pixelio.de

Manufactured and distributed by brebook publishing software (www.brebook.com)

George Smith

The Cassiterides

THE CASSITERIDES:

AN INQUIRY INTO THE

COMMERCIAL OPERATIONS OF THE PHŒNICIANS IN WESTERN EUROPE,

WITH PARTICULAR REFERENCE TO

THE BRITISH TIN TRADE.

BY GEORGE SMITH, LL.D., F.A.S.,

MEMBER OF THE ROYAL ASIATIC SOCIETY,
OF THE ROYAL SOCIETY OF LITERATURE, ETC., ETC.

"THEIR numerous fleets were scattered over the Indian and Atlantic Ocean, and the Tyrian pennant waved at the same time on the coasts of Britain and on the shores of Ceylon."

HEEREN.

LONDON:
LONGMAN, GREEN, LONGMAN, AND ROBERTS.
1863.

LONDON:
PRINTED BY WILLIAM NICHOLS,
46, HOXTON SQUARE.

PREFACE.

The preparation of the following sheets has not arisen from any strong desire to maintain the opinions which they set forth; but from a wish to ascertain and vindicate what is believed to be the truth respecting the subject of which they treat.

This study is not new to the Author. Twenty years ago, when preparing for the publication of his "Religion of Ancient Britain," he was led to a careful examination of the antiquities of our country, and brought to a full conviction that the traditions respecting the early intercourse of the Phœnicians with this island were founded on fact; and that their trading with Cornwall for tin was entitled to be regarded as an established historical truth.

Holding this opinion, he has lately been surprised and felt regret to find eminent authors, for whose learning and talents he has sincere respect, allude in several recent works to this Phœnician intercourse with Britain as a groundless tradition,—a notion which must pass away before a fair historical investigation of the subject. The expression of these doubts, however, has not been accompanied by such historical evidence as proves that the old and prevalent opinion is unworthy of confidence, nor is it shown by what other means the ancient tin markets of Tyre and Egypt were supplied.

In these circumstances the Author has renewed his acquaintance with the subject, and has carefully considered all that has been said on the other side; and, finding his former convictions not only unshaken, but greatly strengthened, by the inquiry, has been induced to put forth the following brief essay, which, if it does nothing toward removing the doubts of those who are sceptical as to the ancient Phœnicians having visited Cornwall for the purchase of tin, may at least serve as an apology for those who, like him, in opposition to such authorities, still entertain old-fashioned opinions on this subject.

TREVU, CAMBORNE,
January 12*th*, 1863.

CONTENTS.

	PAGE
Doubts recently cast on the ancient British tin trade	1
Tin was found in Palestine in very remote times	3
Mr. W. D. Cooley's opinions	4
Was tin brought from the East?	5
The Periplus of Arrian—its testimony	6
The trade of Adooli	7
The trade of Abelites	9
The trade of Mosullon	11
The trade of Opone	12
The trade of Rhapta	13
The trade of Moosa	15
The trade of Kane	16
The trade of Omana	17
The trade of Barbarike	18
The trade of Barugaza	19
The trade of Nelkunda	20
Tin not anciently exported from India	23
Tin exported from Egypt to the East	25
The situation of Tarshish	27
Phœnician colonies	29
Cyprus and Rhodes	30
Crete and Sicily	32
Malta, Sardinia, and Corsica	35

CONTENTS.

	PAGE
Gades, on the coast of Spain	37
Antiquity of Sidon	39
Perfection of the Phœnician navy	41
Date of the building of Gades	43
The quantity of tin found in Spain	46
Geography of the Cassiterides	51
The Belgæ in Britain	55
Tin not anciently carried across Gaul	57
Ezekiel on the tin trade	58
Herodotus on the Cassiterides	59
Julius Cæsar on Britain	60
Diodorus on the Phœnicians and their Trade with Britain	62
Strabo on Gades and Britain	66
Pliny on Spain and Britain—their mines and metal trade	68
Observations on Herodotus	74
Remarks on the account of Cæsar	76
Notes on Diodorus and Strabo	78
Remarks on the statement of Pliny	80
Antiquity of Phœnician commerce	85
Celebrity of their manufactures	87
Devotion to commerce, the ruling spirit of Phœnicia	89
The Tyrian Hercules	94
His extensive success	97
Legends of Melkarth	98
Inventions ascribed to Hercules	100
Phœnician conquest of Tartessus	103
Phœnician settlement in Gaul	105
Monumental remains of Phœnicia in Western Europe	109
Productions and commerce of Gades	110

CONTENTS.

	PAGE
Phœnician trade with Britain	112
Origin and emigrations of the Belgæ	115
Grote on the commerce of Phœnicia	117
Immense profits of this trade	119
Ezekiel on the commerce of Phœnicia	120
Phœnician rapine and violence	123
Assyrian aggression on Western Asia	125
Rise and progressive power of Carthage	127
The Phocean Greeks—their commercial and maritime energy	129
Tyre besieged by Nebuchadnezzar	130
The "*Ora Maritima*" of Avienus	134
The voyage and character of Pytheas	136
The knowledge the ancients had of Britain	140
Decline of the power of Phœnicia	143
Carthage succeeds to Phœnician influence and commerce in the West	145
Commercial prosperity of Massilia	146
Tin carried across Gaul	149
The result of our inquiry	151
Conclusion	153

NOTE.—*In reference to the sketch, on page 46, showing the relative quantities of mineral ground worked in Spain.*

It is stated, on page 46, that these quantities are exclusive of the Government Mines. We accordingly made further inquiry as to whether the Spanish Government does at present work any tin mines, and whether any information could be obtained as to the production of tin, in Spain, in ancient times. The information received from the Government Engineers, at the College of Mines in Madrid, is to the following effect :—
" I cannot learn that Spain ever produced any quantity of this metal. The Government do not work any mines of tin. The quantity being produced at present is very small, chiefly by streamers; or rather labourers, while out of their regular employment, search some of the rivers near the granite hills in Galicia and in Zamora. I cannot learn that there is any tin mining in the country." This communication was received too late to be inserted in its proper place.

THE CASSITERIDES.

For many ages it was currently believed that the Cassiterides were either a part of Britain or islands contiguous to its coast; and that the tin supplied to the East was brought direct from them by Phœnician merchants. This opinion is still received as an established fact, by great numbers of well-informed persons in this country and abroad.

But, recently, great doubt has been raised on these allegations; and a growing scepticism avowed by several intelligent writers. Among others, Mr. W. D. Cooley, in his "History of Maritime and Inland Discovery," and Sir G. Cornewall Lewis, in the "Historical Survey of the Astronomy of the Ancients," have spoken strongly against the probability of a very early direct intercourse between the Phœnicians and Britain.

The problem, therefore, remains to be solved; and we are desirous of making a brief yet complete investigation of the subject.

Questions of this kind do not admit of very clear and ample proof. This tin trade was begun and carried on in remote times,—indeed, before the age of authentic history commenced; and by a people who have left neither literary nor monumental memorials of their doings. We must, therefore, be content with such scattered and unconsecutive evidence as it may be possible to collect.

Some facts may be mentioned *in limine*, respecting which no doubt can exist. Tin was known on the eastern coast of the Mediterranean in the most ancient times. It was found among the spoils of the Midianites in the days of Moses.* The Greeks used it before the Trojan war, to mix with copper for the manufacture of armour and weapons. It is, indeed, an undoubted fact, that tin is mentioned in the most ancient authors, neither as a rare nor as a very precious metal.† It is also certain, that this metal was not a product of Phœnicia, Syria, or Judea. The great marts of Tyre and Egypt must therefore have been supplied either by overland or maritime transit. A

---

* Numbers xxxi. 22.

† "Commerce and Navigation of the Ancients. By W. Vincent, D.D.," vol. i., p. 308.

fair presumption in favour of the latter mode is, that it was found in the greatest abundance among the Phœnicians, who were the most extensive and successful commercial navigators of ancient times. Thus far our way is plain. On these points no real difference of opinion is entertained. Here arises the first question to be solved. Was tin, in the earlier ages, brought to Sidon and Tyre from the East, or the West? from India, or from Spain and Britain?

Mr. Cooley has authoritatively decided this question. It may be regarded as set at rest, so far as his decision has weight. He writes, "There can be no difficulty in determining the country from which tin first arrived in Egypt. That metal has been in all ages a principal export of India: it is enumerated as such by Arrian, who found it abundant in the ports of Arabia, at a time when the supplies of Rome flowed chiefly through that channel. The tin mines of Banca are, probably, the richest in the world. But tin was unquestionably brought from the West at a later period." * This *dictum*, and other statements of the author, have such influence on an eminent reviewer, that he observes,

* "Maritime and Inland Discovery," vol. i., p. 131.

"The cherished tradition that the Phœnicians traded direct to Cornwall in ships, is one which, in our judgment, will not endure searching criticism. Many years ago, in his excellent compendium on 'Maritime and Inland Discovery,' Mr. W. D. Cooley exhibited elaborate and, to us, convincing arguments to show the extreme improbability, not to say incredibility, of this tradition." *

If we felt disposed to receive this opinion of Mr. Cooley with implicit faith, we should be bound to consider the vast distance of time which the authority he cites is made retrospectively to cover. He refers to the Periplus of Arrian, which Dean Vincent, after a careful and learned scrutiny, has attributed to the tenth year of Nero, or A.D. 64. According to Hales, the Israelites crossed the Jordan about B.C. 1608. So that tin was known and used in Palestine about seventeen centuries before Arrian wrote. We are of opinion that in placing such a work before his readers, as proof that tin *at first* came to Egypt from India; the fact that the work on which he relied as an authority was written above sixteen hundred years after its introduction and use, ought to have been stated.

* "London Quarterly Review," No. xxxvii., p. 18.

We will not, however, urge this objection. We do not believe that the traffic with the East greatly changed even in this long period. And if, as is alleged, tin was in the days of Arrian extensively brought from India to Egypt and Palestine, we freely admit that there would be a strong probability of its having been an article of commerce between the two countries for a long period,—although, even in that case, we should not allow its priority over the tin trade of the West, without very careful inquiry into the circumstances of the traffic in very ancient times.

The contents of the Periplus do not justify these allegations. They are, we regret to say, the most remarkable we remember to have seen. We will not anticipate the judgment which the reader shall have an opportunity of forming for himself. The details of the traffic, furnished in this ancient work, are so curious, and so little known, that we will transcribe the substance of the account from the pages of Dr. Vincent. Before doing this, it will be necessary to observe, that the author of the Periplus was not the Arrian of Nicomedia in Bithynia, who wrote a Life of Alexander the Great, and other works; but a merchant navigator of Alexandria in Egypt, who had himself made several commercial voyages from the head of the Red Sea, to the coasts of Africa, as far as the tenth degree of south latitude, and around Arabia and India to the neighbourhood of Ceylon. The information which he thus acquired respecting the geography, navigation, and commerce of those countries, he collected and published under the title of "The Periplus of the Erythrean Sea." "This work," Dean Vincent says, "contains the best account of the commerce carried on from the Red Sea, and coast of Africa, to the East Indies, during the time that Egypt was a province of the Roman Empire." *

The Periplus is divided into two parts. The first treats of the commercial intercourse carried on between Egypt and the eastern coast of Africa. We direct attention to this section, and, excluding all other matter, however inviting, confine our account to a record of the several ports or marts; a list of Exports and Imports of which is furnished.

Adooli, or Aduli, is placed about sixteen degrees north latitude. It is believed to be the same with the bay and harbour of Masuah, so well known by the accounts of the Jesuits, and

* "Commerce and Navigation of the Ancients in the Indian Ocean," vol. ii., p. 3.

of Bruce, as the only proper entrance to Abyssinia. At this port we are told the Exports were ivory, and horns of the rhinoceros.

The Imports:—Cloth, with the nap on, of Egyptian manufacture, for the Barbarian market.
  Robes, made up, the manufacture of Arsinoë or Suez.
  Single cloths dyed, in imitation of those of superior quality.
  Linen, supposed to be from the Latin *linteum*.
  Cloth, striped or fringed.
  Glass, or crystal.
  Porcelain, made at Diospolis, in Egypt, in imitation of the Oriental.
  White copper, for ornaments, and for coin. Ramusio supposes it to contain gold. Gold, by the ounce, is still the medium of commerce, not coined, but exchanged by weight or in the parcel. There seems some allusion to this in the Periplus, where the expression is, εἰς συγκοπὴν ἀντὶ νομίσματος, "cut into pieces so as to pass for money."
  Brass, for culinary vessels, for bracelets, and

ornaments of the legs, still worn in Abyssinia.*

Iron, for spear heads, to hunt the elephants, &c., and for weapons of all sorts.

Hatchets.

Adzes.

Knives, daggers or *kanjars*.

Drinking vessels of brass, large and round.

Denarii, specie for the use of merchants resident in the country. The term proves the currency to be Roman.

Wine, Laodieêan, *i. e.*, Syrian and Italian.

Oil, but in no great quantity.

Gold plate ⎱ According to the fashion of
Silver plate ⎰ the country, and as presents, or for the use of the king.

Watch coats, camp cloaks.

Coverlids, plain.

,, of no great value.

,, not many.

Iron, of Indian temper or manufacture.

Indian cottons, wide and plain; perhaps blue Surat cottons, still common in Abyssinia.

Cotton, for stuffing couches, mattresses, &c.

Sashes, still an article in great request.

Coverlids.

* See Bruce, vol. iii., p. 54.

Cotton cloth, of the colour of the mallows flower.

Muslins, in no great quantity.

Gum lac; but Salmasius thinks it the colour of a cloth or cotton.*

No one can fail to see the business character of this list. It is precisely such an inventory as a merchant would make for his guidance in subsequent transactions with this country. The further accounts are precisely similar.

The next commercial mart, of which the Periplus speaks, is Abalites, close to the Straits of Bab-el-Mandeb. This was a road or bay, not a port or harbour; the goods being conveyed to and from the ships in boats or rafts.

The EXPORTS from this place are :—
Gums, odoriferous gums.
Ivory, in small quantity.
Tortoise-shell.
Myrrh, in very small quantity, but of the finest sort.

The IMPORTS :—
Flint glass of various sorts.
Dipse, rob of grapes, called pacmc, and

* DEAN VINCENT, vol. ii., p. 116.

doushab: it is used as a sauce, or relish, and mixed with water as a drink.

Cloths, for the Barbarine coast, of various sorts, with the nap on.

Corn.

Wine.

Tin, in small quantity.*

Malaô, about eighty miles further south, EXPORTS myrrh and frankincense, thus, or olibanum of Adel.

Cinnamon, cassia lignea.

Cinnamon, of inferior sorts.

The gum cancamus.

Tila, sesamum, carried to Arabia. But see Pliny, xii., 8, who calls it an aromatic from India: the bark red, the root large. The bark used in dysenteries.

Slaves, a few.

The IMPORTS are such as are specified in the preceding list, and in addition:—

Jackets.

Cloaks, or blanketing, manufactured at Arsinoë or Suez, with the nap on, and dyed.

Brass or copper, prepared to imitate gold.

Iron.

* DEAN VINCENT, vol. ii., p. 127.

Specie, gold and silver, but in no great quantity.*

Mosullon, written Mossylon by Pliny, is our next station; it is found rather more than half way from the Straits to the Aromata promontory, the present Cape Guardafui. This was the grand mart of the ancients on this coast.

Its EXPORTS were :—
- Cinnamon, of an inferior quality, and in great quantities; for which reason, vessels of a larger sort are wanted at this mart.
- Fragrant gums.
- Gums or drugs.
- Tortoise-shell, of small size, and in no great quantity.
- Incense, in less quantities, or inferior to that of Moondus.
- Frankincense, from ports farther east.
- Ivory.
- Myrrh, in small quantities.

The IMPORTS are the same as have been already specified, with others peculiar to the place :—

* DEAN VINCENT, vol. ii., p. 129.

Silver plate, or plated.
Iron, but in less quantity.
Flint glass.*

The Periplus names many other places, farther south, on the coast, where commercial operations are carried on, without giving fresh lists of exports and imports; the difference being so slight as not to require mention.

At Opone, we are told, the IMPORTS are the same as at the preceding marts; but

The EXPORTS are given, as :—
  Cinnamon, particularized as native.
  Fragrant gums, or odours; but possibly a species of cinnamon.
  Cinnamon, of inferior quality.
  Slaves, of a superior sort, and principally for the Egyptian market.
  Tortoise-shell, in great abundance, and of superior quality.

At this port, mention is made of a voyage which took place annually between the coast of India and this part of Africa,—undoubtedly by the monsoon. The cargoes specified are

* DEAN VINCENT, vol. ii., p. 135.

precisely such as would be still imported from Guzerat and Concan.

Corn.
Rice.
Butter, that is, ghee.
Oil of sesamum.
Cotton, in the web, and in the flock, for stuffing.
Sashes.
Honey, from the cane, called SUGAR.*

Several other commercial harbours are named, as we proceed southward on the coast; but the next list refers to Rhapta, an important port at about nine degrees south latitude, the furthest point to which the author of the Periplus sailed, in exploring African commerce :—

The EXPORTS from this place are :—
Ivory, in great quantity, but of inferior quality to that obtained at Adooli from Abyssinia.
Rhinoceros, the horn.
Tortoise-shell, of a good sort, but inferior to that of India.

* DEAN VINCENT, vol. ii., pp. 152, 153.

A shell for ornament; but the term is dubious.

The IMPORTS :—
Javelins, more especially such as are the actual manufacture of Moosa.
Hatchets or bills.
Knives, Awls.
Crown glass of various sorts.

Thus closes the information furnished by this interesting record concerning the character of the commerce between Egypt and the several ports on the eastern coast of Africa.

We now direct our attention to the second part of the Periplus, which treats of the trade that existed between Alexandria, Arabia, and India. In this statement we follow the same guide, Dean Vincent, who places before us all the information afforded by the Periplus, supplemented by much more that he has collected from other sources.

The first port mentioned in this account is Moosa, which is just within the straits of Bab-el-Mandeb, on the east shore of the Red Sea.

The EXPORTS from this place are :—

Myrrh of the best quality.

Stacte, or gum.

White stones. Alabaster: with a variety of other articles.

The IMPORTS:—

Purple cloth; fine and ordinary.

Clothes made up in the Arabian fashion, with sleeves, plain and common, and mixed or dappled.

Saffron.

Cyperus. Aromatic rush.

Muslins.

Cloaks.

Quilts, a small assortment; some plain, and others adapted to the fashion of the country.

Sashes, embroidered, or of different shades.

Perfumes.

Specie, for the market, or in considerable quantity.

Wine and corn, not much. The country produces some corn, and a good deal of wine.*

Kane, a port on the coast of Arabia, to the East of the Straits of Bab-el-Mandeb, is spoken of as a place of considerable trade, subject to Eleasus, king of the Incense Country. The

* DEAN VINCENT, vol. ii., p. 316.

Exports are the natural products of the country, frankincense and aloes.

From this mart there was an established intercourse with the countries eastward, that is, with Barugáza, Seindi, Oman, and Persis; so that there was a considerable importation from Egypt, consisting of the following articles:—

A small quantity of wheat.
Wine.
Clothes for the Arabian market.
    ,, common sort.
    ,, plain.
    ,, mixed or adulterated, in great quantities.
Brass.
Tin.
Coral.
Storax, a resin.

And many other articles, the same as are usually imported at Moosa. Besides these also there are brought,

Plate, wrought, and
Specie for the king.
Horses.
Carved images.
Plain cloth, of a superior quality.*

* Dean Vincent, vol. ii., p. 336.

Our author mentions several other places, and notices the pearl fishery of the Persian Gulf; but gives no other catalogue of Exports and Imports relating to Arabia. Our next information of this kind describes the traffic at Omana in Gadrosia, a port not many leagues from Cape Jask, at the mouth of the Persian Gulf.

The EXPORTS from this place were :—
  Pearl in great quantities, but of an inferior sort.
  Purple.
  Cloth for the natives.
  Wine.
  Dates in large quantities.
  Gold.
  Slaves.

The IMPORTS.
  Brass.
  Sandal-wood.
  Wood squared.
  Horn.
  Ebony in round sticks.*

We are now brought to Barbarikè, at the

* DEAN VINCENT, vol. ii., p. 379.

mouth of the Indus. The EXPORTS from this port are :—

    Costus, a spice.
    Bdellium, a gum.
    Yellow dye.
    Spikenard.
    Emeralds or green stones.
    Sapphires.
    Furs from China.
    Cottons.
    Silk thread.
    Indigo, or perhaps Indian ink.

The IMPORTS.

    Clothing, plain and in considerable quantity.
    Clothing, mixed.
    Cloth. Cottons very fine, or larger in the warp than the woof.
    Topazes.
    Coral.
    Storax.
    Frankincense.
    Glass vessels.
    Plate.
    Specie.
    Wine.*

---

* DEAN VINCENT, vol. ii., p. 390.

Barugáza in the Gulf of Cambay is the next commercial station, the traffic of which is detailed. This was not only an important port; but was also the *entrepôt* for the commerce of Ozènè, an inland city, which lay some distance eastward of the port, and was the capital of the country. The EXPORTS from this place were :—

Onyx stones.
Porcelain.
Fine muslins.
Muslins of the colour of mallows.
A large quantity of ordinary cottons.

The following articles are also spoken of as passing through Ozènè, for export from Barugaza, viz. :—

Spikenard.
Costus.
Bdellium.
Ivory.
Onyx stone.
Myrrh.
Box-thorn.
Cottons of all sorts.
Silk.
Mallow-coloured cotton.
Silk thread.
Long pepper.

The IMPORTS at Barugáza are:—
  Wine:—Italian in preference to all other.
  ,,   Laodicean, Syrian.
  ,,   Arabian. *Query*, palm or toddy.
Brass.
Tin.
Lead.
Coral.
Topazes.
Cloth,—plain.
  ,,   mixed, of all sorts.
Variegated or fine sashes, half a yard wide.
Storax.
Sweet lotus.
White glass.
Ore of Cinnabar.
Stibium for tinging the eyes.
Ordinary perfumes, or unguents, and in no great quantity.*

The next port, Baráki or Nelkunda, is believed to be the extent of the personal voyaging of the author of the Periplus in this direction. It lies about midway between Goa and Cape Comorin.

The EXPORTS are:—

* DEAN VINCENT, vol. ii., p. 409.

Pepper, in great quantity, which grows only in this one place, and which is called the pepper of Cottonara.

Pearls, in quantity and quality superior to others.

Ivory.

Fine silks.

Gapanic spikenard : it is usually read Gangetic.

Betel.

,, from the countries farther to the East.

All sorts of transparent or precious stones.

Diamonds.

Jacinths. Rubies.

Tortoise-shell from the Golden Island, (either Khrusê ? or Maldives ?) and another sort taken in the islands which lie off the coast of Limürikê (the Laccadives).

The principal IMPORTS :—

Great quantities of specie.

Topazes.

A small assortment of plain cloth.

Fine cloths of different colours.

Stibium for colouring the eyes.

Coral.

White glass.

Brass.
Tin.
Lead.
A small quantity of wine.
Cinnabar.
Orpiment.
Corn. Only for the use of the ship's company: the merchants do not sell it.*

At the risk of being tedious, we have placed the details of this traffic before the reader, and for this simple reason,—that it does not supply what is so frequently found in investigations of this sort, namely, conjectures and opinions, but sterling matters of fact. Here we have set before us, with all the particularity of a modern invoice, the exact articles of traffic between Egypt, Ceylon, and Africa, eighteen hundred years ago. Were we discussing ancient commerce generally, there would be many and interesting subjects for observation, suggested by these lists. We might notice the sameness of character which the trade with the East has always maintained; and the uniform and continuous demand for specie which the East has always made on the western world. But we are confined to one

* Dean Vincent, vol. ii., p. 469.

section of the subject,—the trade of the ancients in tin. We were sent to the writings of Arrian, and to the ports of Arabia, for proofs that Egypt derived her supplies of this metal from the East. We were told that this "metal has been in all ages a principal export of India,"—that "it is enumerated as such by Arrian." * We ask, in reply, Where does Arrian say this ? When was tin first exported from India ? We can find no such information in Arrian. His profoundly learned translator and commentator has found nothing of the kind. We have ranged over the whole line of Egyptian maritime commerce, as given in its earliest authentic records; but find no trace of tin being carried from the East or the South to that country. We have examined the commerce of the ports of Abyssinia, Arabia, and India. And what has been the result ? We have found, indeed, that tin was known, and recognised as an article of traffic; but that, instead of its coming from the East to Egypt, it has been invariably exported from Egypt to the East.

We have found tin in the great mart of Kane in Arabia; but then we are distinctly told that it was exported from Egypt to that

* Cooley's "Maritime," &c., vol. i., p. 131.

great centre of Arabian commerce, from which the surrounding countries derived their supplies. At Barugaza in the Gulf of Cambay, and at Nelkunda on the coast of Malabar, tin has been found as an element of trade; but in every instance as an export from Egypt. Where, then, we ask, is the proof that this metal had been supplied by India? The commercial operations which we have reviewed embrace the great traffic of the East. We have found articles that must have been supplied from the further parts of India; we have even recorded the sale of furs from China; but we have heard of no supplies of Indian tin. We might show at length, that if there ever was such a trade, it must have existed at this time, and have been carried on by this route.

The supplies of tin at Banca are, we are assured, even now, inexhaustible; so that if these mines had been wrought in the early ages, there must have been an abundance for sale in the times of Arrian. We fully agree with Dr. Vincent, that in the earliest times traffic was chiefly conducted by overland routes; but it is equally true, that generally, and especially in Arabia, this mode of transit has always been dangerous and expensive;

and particularly for a heavy and not very costly commodity, like tin. When gold, specie, and diamonds were sent by sea, tin would not be sent overland. But we need not pursue this argument. The question is settled by one fact. If the merchants of Malabar could have procured tin from the East, they would not have imported it from Egypt.

We are told, it is improbable that the most successful and experienced navigators of their day should sail from Cadiz to Cornwall. Yet those who make this assertion find no difficulty in believing that a people whose practice of navigation is entirely unknown to us should sail twice that distance, from Ceylon to Banca. Those who, in the face of this evidence, assert that tin was in the earliest times procured from the East, and who decry the Phœnician maritime intercourse with Britain, nevertheless speak of the "rashness of modern criticism," as though they alone had employed patient investigation and sound induction on the subject.

The venerable Dean of Westminster—who translated, dissected, and commented on the Periplus of Arrian the merchant, and who rendered a similar service to the account of the Voyage of Nearchus with Alexander's fleet down the Indus, along the coast of Beloochistan to the Persian Gulf, and thence up to Susa, written by the more eminent Arrian—has expressed his opinion on this question. Having added to the knowledge of eastern navigation and commerce acquired by these translations and researches an immense fund of information derived from other sources, he had no doubts in his mind as to the country whence the tin exported to India from Egypt was procured. He says, "Tin was another of the articles enumerated: and if we find this produce of Britain conveyed to Malabar in the earliest period that history can reach, we find the spices of Malabar in Britain in an age when the course of the communication with India was probably as little known as the existence of America. The Venerable Bede, who died in the year A.D. 735, was possessed of pepper, cinnamon, and frankincense. Did no one ever ask the question, how, in that age, these luxuries had been conveyed to Britain, or were treasured in a cell at Weirmouth?"*

But we have no intention of prejudging the question, or of endeavouring to settle it by the authority of a great name. We claim at present simply to have disproved the allegation, that in

* DEAN VINCENT, vol. ii., p. 460.

the time of Arrian and in the earlier ages tin was carried as an article of commerce from India to Egypt. We, on the contrary, maintain, that reasonable proof has been afforded, that until this time India itself was dependent upon Egypt for supplies of tin, as Egypt undoubtedly was on the West of Europe.

The main subject of our investigation is now placed before us in this new phase. We find tin in the early ages abundant in Phœnicia, and a current commodity of commerce at Tyre, B. C. 600.* It was known and used in Palestine at least six hundred years earlier. It was not the product of those countries or of the neighbouring ones, but procured at the later date certainly from Tarshish.† We have to search out this locality, with this one limitation to the range of our inquiry: that although this term may have been sometimes used with a wide range of meaning, and as applicable to different countries; in this case, it cannot refer to India on the East. We have ascertained beyond all doubt, that down to a time long after this the East did not export this metal, but had to procure their supplies of it from the West. The oriental countries are therefore excluded from further inquiry. We must look else-

* Ezek. xxvii. 12. † *Ibid.*

where for the source which supplied this metal to the ancient world.

Tyre being the great emporium of the tin trade, at the date above mentioned, B.C. 600, and Tarshish the country from whence the merchants brought this commodity, we have to ascertain the situation of the mines that produced this metal, and the route by which it reached the Phœnician capital.

As a preliminary to this investigation, it is necessary to remind the reader that, although the period which has been mentioned is so remote, it does not represent the beginning of this commerce, but the time when it had attained its maturity, and when the Phœnicians were in the zenith of their greatness. Greece had just then risen to distinction; her earliest history began but two hundred years before; and Herodotus, the father of her historians, did not appear until another century had elapsed. Rome had been founded about one hundred and fifty years, and was still an unwalled and insignificant Italian town. Yet even at this early period Phœnicia had existed more than sixteen hundred years, and during the far greater portion of that time had been a wealthy commercial nation. These circumstances, in the absence of consecutive historical records, may warrant the admission of circumstantial evidence of a reasonable and conclusive character.

The limited territory which the Phœnicians possessed on the coast of Palestine has been frequently referred to, as insufficient to be the seat of a great and powerful state. But those who have urged this objection have overlooked the important fact, that this people, being devoted to commerce and commercial navigation, as the grand means of their national greatness, sought in extensive colonial establishments a means of support, and appliances for the promotion of their great objects, which no extent of continental soil could supply.

To these colonies we shall have to refer, as the best available means of tracing the progress, extent, and times of Phœnician commercial enterprise. Cyprus is a large and important island, within sixty-five miles of Laodicea, on the Phœnician coast, and is distinctly visible from Mount Cassius. The advantage of this position to a maritime nation is self-evident. It commands the waters of the Levant, the coasts of Syria and Cilicia; it contains many excellent harbours; and, what is of pre-eminent importance in the present consideration, it afforded abundance of excellent timber and every other material for the building and equipment of ships. But if the archives of Tyre, or of Sidon, (for it is more likely that Cyprus was colonized in the times when the parent city was in the ascendant,) contained any records of the establishment of Phœnician settlements on this island, they have long since perished. We have only one or two attesting facts, in proof of an occupation which cannot be doubted. In historic times Cyprus was divided into nine kingdoms; and of these, five are shown by their names and traditions to have had a Phœnician origin. The mention of Cyprus in the Iliad proves, that so early as the time of the Trojan war it was regarded as a powerful state. But the most significant fact is the statement, that Cinyras, king of Cyprus, presented to Agamemnon, when about to sail to the Trojan war, a very curious breastplate, composed of lead, gold, and tin;* thus showing that the

---

* "Next he placed around his breast a corslet which Cinyras once gave him to be a pledge of hospitality. For a great rumour was heard at Cyprus, that the Greeks were about to sail to Troy in ships; wherefore he gave him this, gratifying the king. Ten bars, indeed, (of the corslet,) were

Cyprian colonists possessed the staple commodities and metallurgic skill of the parent state.

Rhodes is inferior in size to Cyprus, but is more fertile, and has excellent harbours. Of its occupation by the Sidonians, Mr. Kenrick, who has fully investigated the subject, observes, "The traces of Phœnician intereourse are numerous; those of colonization are less distinct than in Cyprus, but sufficient to justify the conclusion that the Phœnicians were once predominant in the island." * If we may rely on the curious production of the alleged follower of Idomeneus, Dictys Cretensis, this intercourse of Phœnicia with Rhodes was of a very early date; for he speaks of the expedition led by Memnon to the Trojan war, and which was composed in great part of Ethiopians (or Phœnicians,)† as having landed and settled here.‡ In Crete, also, there are traces of the Phœnicians, although the nearer we

---

of dark cyanus, twelve of gold, and twenty of tin; and three serpents of cyanus stretched towards the neck on each side like unto rainbows."—Literal Translation of HOMER's "Iliad," lib. xi., p. 24. Bohn's Edition.

* KENRICK's "Phœnicia," p. 79.
† *De Bello Trojano*, lib. iv., 4. Amsterdam. 1702.
‡ HERODOTUS, vii., 90.

approach to Greece, the more completely has the later Greek population swept away the remains of ancient Phœnician intercourse. Yet there still remain clear historical proofs of Phœnician colonization. The name of one of the harbours bears some evidence of this fact.* It was celebrated for its mines of gold. A curious incident, recorded by Herodotus, gives countenance to the evident probability that Crete also had been brought under Phœnician influence, or had been in frequent communication with that country. We are told that the inhabitants of the isle of Thera, having consulted the oracle at Delphi as to the removal of a destructive drought with which they were afflicted, were commanded by it to build a city in Libya. Not knowing where this country was, they sent messengers to Crete, to inquire whether any one there knew the place. They found a man who had been in Libya, and who was "a dyer of purple,"—an art in which the Phœnicians were pre-eminent.†

Still farther north, on the mainland, opposite to Samothrace, the Phœnician mining operations were so extensive, that Herodotus speaks of his having seen the works, and says,

* Acts xxvii. 12. † Melpomene, 151.

that a mountain had been effectually levelled by the miners. He observes, that these mines were discovered by the Phœnicians, who were under the direction of Thasus.* Melos, one of the Cyclades, also contained many mineral productions, which must have been very valuable to the Phœnicians. It was rich in alum of superior quality, had inexhaustible mines of sulphur, besides other useful products. Mr. Kenrick places the Phœnician colonization of this island about B.C. 1200.† Without staying to notice many other places which bear witness to the early and persevering enterprise of this wonderful people, we proceed to refer to more distant settlements.

Sicily affords similar evidence of a very early Phœnician occupation, and of this being greatly modified by subsequent circumstances. However ignorant the Greeks might have been of this island, it must have been well known to the Cretans and Phœnicians long before the times of Homer : it commended itself to the attention of the latter people by the abundance and superior quality of its corn, wine, and other productions. At first, they appear to have occupied all the principal promontories; but afterwards, when

* Erato, 47. † "Phœnicia," p. 96.

the Greeks aspired to be a naval power, and multiplied their colonies, it was found inconvenient to defend so many settlements. The Phœnicians accordingly withdrew their people and property from the other localities, and concentrated all their wealth and power at the north-western angle of the island, where, as Thucydides* states, they continued to live in alliance with the Elymi, who occupied a part of that neighbourhood. The concentration of the Phœnicians at this place is by Mr. Kenrick supposed to have occurred about B.C. 736;† and as he calculates from the known times of the Greek movements which occasioned the removal, there can be little doubt of his accuracy. Malta was an island of too much importance to be overlooked by these maritime merchants. We are told by Diodorus " that it is about eight hundred furlongs from Syracuse, is furnished with very good harbours, and that the inhabitants are very rich; for it is full of all sorts of artificers, among whom there are excellent weavers of fine linen. Their houses are very stately and beautiful, adorned with graceful cornices and ornaments in plaster. The inhabitants are a colony of Phœnicians, who,

---

* THUCYDIDES, vi. 2.   † "Phœnicians," p. 106.

trading as merchants as far as the western ocean, resorted to this island on account of its commodious ports and convenient situation for a sea trade; and by the advantage of this place the inhabitants soon became famous for their wealth and merchandise."* As this island was at first a bare rock of limestone, the persevering people who had taken possession of it brought soil from the neighbouring coast of Africa, and carefully provided it with the means of cultivation, until its fertility became proverbial.†

It would be unnecessary, even if it were possible, to notice all the settlements which the Phœnicians formed in the Mediterranean; or it might be shown that Sardinia, Corsica, the Balearic, and other islands, had been more or less occupied by them, and rendered subsidiary to their great commercial purposes and plans. Carthage cannot, with strict propriety, be placed in the category of colonies,‡ although

---

* DIOD. SIC., v., 1.   † OVID. *Fast.*, iii., 567.

‡ "There would seem to be much probability in the conjecture that the city originated in a mere emporium, (or, in modern language, a factory, like that in which the Anglo-Indian empire had its first beginning,) established jointly by the mother city and Utica, on account of the convenience of its position; and that it rose into importance by the natural process of immigration." (DR. SMITH'S " Dictionary

it has been conjectured that its origin was of this character; but it was an important offshoot from the Phœnician stock, and was regarded as such throughout their whole history; so that, as Herodotus informs us, Cambyses, when he had determined to invade Carthage, was obliged to lay aside his design, because the Phœnicians refused to aid him with their navy against their descendants.* Even then it was an admitted fact, that all the Persian navy was unequal to cope with that of Carthage, unless assisted by the Phœnicians. Utica, as already intimated, was also founded on the African continent many years before Carthage, became an important port and city, and long survived its more powerful neighbour.

But, not content with the commerce of this inland sea, Phœnician enterprise passed through the Straits of Hercules, explored the shores of the Atlantic, and formed settlements on the ocean coasts of Africa and Spain. It is

of Geography," vol. i., p. 531.) If any reliance is to be placed on the legend of Dido, it is much more probable that her expedition should sail to a small and rising colony, and take possession of it, than that it should seek an unoccupied part of the coast, and found an entirely new settlement.

* Thalia, 19.

extremely difficult to fix with any precision the origin and progress of this colonization. Its issue in the establishment of an important settlement at Gades or Gadeira (Cadiz) is well known; but it is more than probable that this was not the first attempt to take possession of part of the coast of Spain. The inhabitants of Gades affirmed that their island was not the first place fixed on for a colony. And Strabo* gives countenance to the facts which had thus obtained currency, by the following narrative:—It was reported that the Tyrians were warned by an oracle to send a colony to the Pillars of Hercules, and that the expedition selected for this purpose fixed on a place near Malaga. As the sacrifices offered by them were inauspicious, they returned home for further instructions. A second deputation, sent for the same purpose, passed the straits, and, finding an island dedicated to Hercules, opposite to Huelva, at the confluence of the Odiel and Tinto, they again sacrificed, and again found the appearance of the victims unfavourable. A third expedition fixed on Gadeira.—Although this account is coloured with the superstitions which affected alike the actors in these movements and the historians

* STRABO, iii., 55.

by whom the information has been transmitted to our times, no reasonable doubt can be entertained that it exhibits a series of long-continued endeavours to effect a permanent location on the Spanish soil. Success at last abundantly crowned these persevering efforts. Gades rose to be a most important *entrepôt* of commerce, a large naval establishment, and a very wealthy and flourishing town. Strabo says,* it was second only to Rome in his time; and there was only one city (Padua) in Italy, Rome excepted, which could produce an equal number of citizens of the equestrian order. This was the case, although the limits of the city were small, and a large proportion of the inhabitants were always engaged in navigation or foreign commerce; for, according to the authority already given, Gades equipped and sent to sea, both for the Mediterranean and ocean trade, more and larger vessels than any other port. Of course this refers to the time of Strabo, (B.C. 20,) long after Tyre and Carthage had perished. The Phœnicians also founded Seville, calling it Hispalis; this, too, became a flourishing city.

We have hitherto spoken of these colonies without any regard to the chronological order

* STRABO, iii., 5, 3.

ANTIQUITY OF SIDON.

of their foundation. Indeed, with respect to many of them, it is impossible to specify any date approximating to their first occupation. It seems probable that generally a long-continued commercial intercourse preceded any colonial establishment; and that even when a settlement was made, its progress was so gradual that no date could, with strict propriety, be assigned to it. Yet it is important to trace as nearly as possible the beginning of this remarkable course of commercial arrangements, and the successive foundation of some of the most famous colonies.

The rise of the commercial power of Sidon is lost in its extreme antiquity. It was called the "great Sidon" during the administration of Joshua, B.C. 1600. And not only had it, at this early date, opened up markets for procuring the materials necessary for a vast range of metallic and fibrous manufactures, but it had actually attained, what it must have occupied a long space of time to acquire after these materials had been procured, consummate perfection in all the arts of design, composition, and manipulation. Our limits forbid an enumeration, or we might give a catalogue of the most elegant and costly articles of the times, which emanated from this city.

Yet all this commercial activity had been exercised, and these arts successfully and extensively practised, long before the Trojan war, which may be fixed at about 1200 B.C. Homer, who never names Tyre, celebrates, as being specifically of Sidonian manufacture, the most rare and valuable presents which his kings and heroes received. But Sidon was abandoned, and the arts and power of Phœnicia transferred to Tyre, just a year before the fall of Troy;* so that the rise, progress, and glory of Sidonian navigation, commerce, and manufacture took place before this date. It is true, we have at Tyre to deal with the same people and the same pursuits as at Sidon. Yet the transfer affords an intelligible epoch, which exhibits, in a very striking manner, the long and successful career which the parent city had previously accomplished.

Turning from the foundation and growth of Phœnician cities to the formation of the vast colonial system which the Phœnicians reared up, it is easy to conceive of an aspiring people, with a limited continental territory, taking possession of contiguous islands like Cyprus and Crete; but what progress must have been made in ship-building and in navi-

* JUSTIN, xviii., 3.

gation, before Sardinia or Malta would have been visited from Sidon! Yet this had been accomplished. Inventions so numerous had been devised, and such wonderful progress made in all the various arts employed in the construction and management of large vessels, that the Phœnician navy was for ages the wonder of all beholders. In the *Œconomicus* of Xenophon, a Greek is represented as having said, "The best and most accurate arrangement of things, I think, I ever saw, was when I went to look at the great Phœnician ship. For I saw the greatest quantity of tackling separately disposed in the smallest stowage. You know that a ship comes to anchor or gets under way by means of many wooden instruments, and many ropes, and sails by means of many sails, and is armed with many machines against hostile vessels, and carries about with it many arms for the crew, and all the apparatus which men use in a dwelling-house, for each mess. Besides all this, the vessel is filled with cargo which the owner carries for his profit. And all that I have mentioned lay in not much greater space than would be found in a chamber large enough for ten beds. All things, too, lay in such a way that they did not obstruct one another, so that they needed no one to seek them, could be easily got together, and there were no knots to be untied, and cause delay, if they were suddenly wanted for use." *

But these arrangements must have been rendered very perfect, and their science and practice of navigation much beyond what is usually ascribed to them, before they would attempt to explore the ocean, and to form settlements on its shores. It is a well-known fact, that the earliest Greek writers regarded Sicily and the coast of Italy as on the extreme verge of the world; bordering on the regions of endless night. Yet these adventurous people dared to leave these shores far behind them, and to pass the straits into the vast ocean beyond. We have seen that the first attempts to colonize the west coast of Europe were not successful; but they were repeated until the end was attained. There can be little doubt that Tartessus had been often visited, and a valuable commerce established there, long before any attempt was made to occupy a part of the coast.

And yet the dates of the early Phœnician settlements, as far as they are ascertained, are very remote. Carthage is believed to have

* Kenrick's "Phœnicia," p. 235.

DATE OF THE BUILDING OF GADES. 43

been founded about B.C. 813; Utica, according to Strabo, was built two hundred and eighty-seven years before Carthage, which places the foundation of that colony B.C. 1100. It is stated by Velleius Paterculus, in his Compendium of Roman History, that "at this time, about eighty years after Troy was taken,.........a fleet of the Tyrians, then very powerful at sea, founded the city of Gades, in the remotest coast of Spain, at the extremity of one part of the world, and on an island surrounded by the ocean, divided from the continent only by a very narrow strait. By the same people, also, a few years afterwards, Utica, in Africa, was built." * According to Pliny, this last-mentioned city was built eleven hundred years before our era; for, writing in B.C. 77 or 78, he observes: "The temple of Apollo at Utica is equally celebrated; there we see beams of cedar still in existence, and in just the same condition in which they were when erected in the first building of that city, eleven hundred and seventy-eight years ago." † Pomponius Mela, also, having mentioned the temple of Hercules, at Gades, adds, that the foun-

* VELLEIUS PATERCULUS, i., 2.
† PLINY, *Nat. Hist.*, xvi., 79 (40).

dation of the colony was from "the time of Troy."*

We have set down the fall of the Phrygian capital at about B.C. 1200, the most reliable authorities placing it near that date;† and this conclusion makes the era of the building of Gades sufficiently in harmony with the decision of Mr. Kenrick, who, having most elaborately investigated the whole subject, says, "The first event in the history of the Phœnicians to which a date can be assigned, is the foundation of Gades in the twelfth century B.C." There was therefore the long preceding commercial exploration of Western Europe, the extensive traffic with Tartessus, the three successive attempts at colonization, of which we have spoken; and all this took place before the establishment of Gades, about or soon after B.C. 1200. But it will be seen, that this is just the date that the circumstances of the case require. Tin must have been largely imported into Phœnicia at least as early as B.C. 1500; and to this conclusion all the accounts tend. If tin was used in

* POMPONIUS MELA, iii., 6.
† Eratosthenes and Apollodorus place the fall of Troy, B.C. 1183; Dionysius, B.C. 1184: and the Parian Marble, B.C. 1209.—CLINTON's *Fasti Hellenici*, vol. i., pp. 129-132.

articles of the most elaborate design and manufacture prior to the Trojan war; then, as there was no supply of this metal, as far as we can learn, from the East, there must have been a known market from whence it was procured. All our sources of information agree, therefore, in placing the Phœnician tin market at Gades, for several centuries before B.C. 1100, when it may be regarded as in great prosperity.

The question which arises out of these facts, is simply this: Whence was this market supplied? We are told that tin in ancient times was abundant in Spain. We are all well aware, that silver was found plentifully there. But we have never seen any satisfactory evidence, that tin in any considerable quantities was produced in that country.*

---

* The most remarkable feature in tin mining seems to be the enduring character of the mines. Wherever tin has been produced in any considerable quantities within the range of authentic history, there it is still abundantly found. In Banca, we are told, the supply is inexhaustible; and Cornwall can now supply as large a quantity annually as it ever could. On this principle, we have inquired as to the supply of tin at present in Spain; and our informant, who has been some years in active employment in the principal mining districts of that country, says, "I have never met a tin miner nor a tin streamer in Spain; all the tin I have seen exposed for sale had been imported from England."

Nor do any of the accounts or traditions that have come down to us indicate as much. Tarshish supplied Tyre with tin; but the *Cassiterides* are spoken of as the place where the commodity was mined; and the Cassiterides have generally been regarded as the

Another fact bearing on this point is important. Silver is generally found in contact with lead, seldom or never with tin ores. In ancient times, it is well known, that Spain produced abundance of silver. The *Revissa Minera* of 1860 showed the quantity of ground let out to miners throughout the whole of Spain to search for minerals of all kinds. The quantities then in the possession of miners for this purpose is given in the annexed sketch, from which it will be seen, that while the surface occupied for lead mining is decidedly the largest, the appropriation for search after tin is all but the smallest; the whole surface bored for tin mining throughout the whole of Spain being little more than one square mile.

SPAIN.
1859.
S.H.—

—SCALE—
VARAS 10 100
N.B. A VARA IS 35 ENGLISH INCHES

SURFACE GRANTED FOR THE SEARCH OF MINERALS, IN ALL SPAIN TO END OF THE YEAR 1859.
(THE GOVERNMENT MINES NOT INCLUDED.)

a	b	c	d	e	f	g	h	i	j	k
NICKEL COBALT	QUICKSILVER	TIN	MANGANESE	ARSENIC	SILVER	GOLD	IRON	ZINC	LIGNITE	COPPER	COAL	LEAD

south-western part of the British islands. Even Sir G. Cornewall Lewis, who cannot believe that Phœnician ships sailed to this island, is constrained to say, "It cannot be doubted that Britain was the country from which the tin sold by the Phœnicians to the Greeks was chiefly procured." *

But we are told that it is "incredible" that the Phœnician vessels should have visited Cornwall for the purposes of trade. Let us consider this objection. Let it have all the weight to which it is entitled. We only desire the subject to be *fairly* considered. It is alleged that the distance is great. We admit it. The distance from Cadiz to Cornwall in a straight course is about one thousand miles; and, following the coast, as probably ancient navigators usually did, considerably more. But then let it be remembered, that we ascribe this voyage to men who had built a city, as a colonial settlement, two thousand five hundred miles from their native shores; to a people so familiarized with maritime commerce, as to have established *depôts* on most of the islands and on every shore of the Mediterranean! Is it reasonable to suppose, that Gades would have been built at the extreme distance to

* "Historical Survey," &c., p. 451.

which their commerce reached? Let it be conceded for a moment, that the tin fields of Cornwall had become known to the Phœnicians; where could they have had a colonial station more advantageously situated for prosecuting this intercourse, than at Cadiz? There was a mart for valuable commodities at hand, and a fine harbour with every convenience for repairing or refitting their vessels. And from thence to Cornwall was a shorter voyage than from Tyre to Malta, Carthage, or Sicily, which they were performing continually. It is well known, that the shores of the bay round to Cape St. Vincent were regarded as Phœnician soil, and that this Cape was spoken of as "the sacred promontory." We confess that we are puzzled to find the difficulty which has staggered so many eminent writers. If we were ascribing this discovery and commercial navigation to persons who had no means of transit on the water but British coracles, or Indian boats, sewn together with strips of bark, or hides, we should expect the idea to be rejected. But when it is attributed to a people who had a navy, and naval skill to go to and fro with impunity over the stormy Ægean, who could dare without fear the tempests of the middle Mediterranean, and even launch on the wide

Atlantic, we think we are neither unreasonable nor rash in ascribing to the Phœnicians direct naval intercourse with Cornwall.

The extent to which Phœnician commerce was carried is startling to modern ears in every respect. Four days' sail from Gades, in the waters of the Atlantic, we are told, the people of Gades established a fishery for conger-eels and tunnies, which were cured in a manner that rendered them luxuries at Athenian tables.* So valued was this article, that when the Carthaginians succeeded to the trade after the fall of Tyre, they prohibited the export of it to any other place. And although patent on the pages of their Bibles, perhaps most readers will feel some surprise at being told, that the Tyrians had a fish market at Jerusalem.† The mackerel was also a very important element of merchandise. From this fish, the people of Carteia ‡ prepared a sauce which brought fabulous prices, equal to those of the richest perfumes. As salt was a commodity imported into Britain, in return for the tin exported from thence, it does not appear to be improbable that Cornish fish, as well as

* KENRICK'S "Phœnicia," p. 225.
† Nehemiah xiii. 16.
‡ A place five miles west of Gibraltar.

tin, was taken from thence by the Phœnicians, and carried to distant markets.

It is an admitted fact, that the Phœnician voyagers sailed to the south of the Straits of Hercules, far enough to discover the Canary Islands. These were called by the Greeks the Islands of the Blessed, and by the Latins the Fortunate Islands. Yet, although this is a part of undoubted history, learned men think it improbable and incredible that they should have sailed a little further from Cadiz, to trade with a country so rich in various important commodities as the south-west parts of England.

It is further objected, that the accounts which are given of the Cassiterides are indefinite and contradictory. These objections may be given as diligently summed up by Mr. Cooley. He says, "The name *Cassiterides* (Tin Islands) is evidently but an epithet, implying the want of particular acquaintance with the countries thus vaguely denominated. But as geographers feel peculiar pleasure in fixing the position of every wandering name, the title of 'Tin Islands' was inconsiderately bestowed by Greek and Roman writers, at one time on real islands in which there was no tin, at another on imaginary islands

GEOGRAPHY OF THE CASSITERIDES.

near the coasts abounding in that metal. Almost all these accounts refer the *Cassiterides* to the coast of Spain. Some writers place them many days' sail in the western ocean; others, nearly opposite to Corunna; but they are never mentioned (with a single exception) with respect to their distance from the coast of Britain; a circumstance which, to those acquainted with the ancient system of navigation, must be a convincing argument that the *Cassiterides* were not the Scilly Islands. Cæsar and Tacitus, though they mention the gold, silver, and pearls of Britain, take hardly any notice of its tin mines. Pliny, moreover, after discussing all the accounts relating to the *Cassiterides*, concludes, that these islands had but a fabulous existence; and observes, that tin in his time was brought from Galicia."*

We have copied this long extract, because we wish to consider the subject in all its bearings. In doing this, there are some questions which we can scarcely refrain from putting on this passage. Why does the term *Cassiterides* imply the want of acquaintance with the place so denominated? Why, any more than the Gold Coast of Africa? The

* "Maritime and Inland Discovery," vol. i., p. 132.

terms alike simply indicate the principal product of the country : the name, *per se*, neither intimates an acquaintance with the position of the place, nor the absence of this knowledge. It might in the case of the "Tin Islands" have been given, as it was by Herodotus, with a very limited knowledge of the locality. But that says nothing as to the knowledge of those who applied the term in the first instance.

If Greek and Roman writers used the term *Cassiterides*, without any definite acquaintance with the geography referred to, it is excusable; seeing that this trade must have been opened five hundred years before Grecian history began, and still longer before the foundation of Rome was laid. It is also objected, that this term is sometimes applied to islands where there is no tin, and at other times to places which are not islands. If the former part of this remark is intended to apply to Scilly, it is incorrect: Scilly has produced tin, although in modern times not in large quantities. The latter part of the observation has been answered by its author. He knew that the Hebrew, Phœnician, and cognate languages had no terms which distinctly specified islands, peninsulas, &c.;

one word being used to signify islands, sea-coasts, and even remote countries. In those languages, the whole coast of Cornwall and Devonshire might be termed island or islands. Then, again, it is mentioned as contradictory, that these *Cassiterides* are by some writers placed many days' sail in the western ocean; and by others, nearly opposite to Corunna! But what is there contradictory in this statement? Let the reader look on a map of western Europe. He will find Corunna a short distance to the north-east of Cape Finisterre, on the south-west extremity of the Bay of Biscay; and the coast soon afterwards runs in a direction nearly east and west. If a vessel, therefore, was to sail from Corunna eastward, on this coast, about one hundred and twenty or one hundred and thirty miles; and then, starting exactly at right angles with the line of coast, should sail direct north, it would reach the Mount's Bay, in the south-west extremity of Britain, and the centre of the tin mines; the distance from this point, on the southern shore of the Bay of Biscay, to Cornwall, being somewhat more than four hundred miles, which would be several days' sail in the western ocean. It is not just to construe the language of ancient writers under the false impression, that the western coast of the European continent is a straight line, running from north to south, and that an island, to be opposite any given point, must lie to the west of it. To be opposite a coast, is to be in such a position, that, leaving that coast at right angles, you will reach the place so described. Cornwall is in this sense nearly opposite Corunna; that is, it is directly opposite a point about one hundred miles from Corunna, and lies in that direction, several days' sail in the western ocean. It may be fully admitted that the Greek and Latin writers had no very clear knowledge of the *Cassiterides*. It is well known that the Phœnicians were in advance of every other nation in these discoveries and pursuits, and that they endeavoured as much as possible to keep the knowledge of them to themselves. In such circumstances, obscurity in the classic accounts is rather a proof of truth and genuineness, than the reverse.

But the grand objection to the Phœnician intercourse with Britain is the allegation that the tin trade was carried on overland through Gaul to Marseilles. As it is an undoubted fact that some of this traffic, at a certain period, did take this course, it is necessary to look carefully into circumstances and dates, that we may ascertain the truth as nearly as possible.

It must, then, be remembered, that all our information respecting the commerce of Britain with Gaul refers to times subsequent to the location of the Belgæ on the island. Cæsar informs us, that when he invaded Britain, the inland parts of the island were inhabited by the aborigines, but that the sea-coast was "peopled with Belgians." "These," he observes, "passing over from different parts, still retain the names of the several states whence they are descended." * They had established an active commercial intercourse with their Gallic kinsmen on the Continent. One reason or pretext which Cæsar assigned for the invasion of this country, was, "that in all his wars with the Gauls, the enemies of the commonwealth had ever received assistance from" Britain.† The commerce carried on by those kindred people, on each side of the Channel, was so extensive, that the merchants who conducted it were many, and well known. So much so, indeed, that when Cæsar meditated his invasion, he called a meeting of these merchants, hoping to learn from them "the nature of the inhabitants, and acquaint himself

* "Wars," v., 10.   † Ibid., iv., 28.

with the coast, harbours, and landing-places, to all which the Gauls were perfect strangers," as, he says, "scarcely any but merchants resort to that island." * But the merchants seemed to think it not likely to promote their interests to be communicative. Cæsar did not procure the desired information. But the Britons, nevertheless, learned from them the designs of Cæsar, and sent ambassadors to Gaul to meet him with offers of submission. Of the trade carried on by these merchants, Cæsar says, " They use brass money, and iron rings of a certain weight. The provinces remote from the sea produce tin; and those upon the coast, iron; but the latter in no great quantity. Their brass is all imported." † From this account we do not think it will be generally inferred, that, prior to Cæsar's wars, the tin trade of Cornwall was carried across the Channel, and over Gaul to Marseilles.

But, however this may have been, the trade of which we speak began at least as early as B.C. 1200, and lasted for more than a thousand years. Now Marseilles was built by the Phocean Greeks shortly before the expulsion of that people from their native city, by Harpagus, the Persian general, about B.C. 600. When

* "Wars," iv., 28. † *Ibid.*, v., 10.

we consider, therefore, the isolated position of the inhabitants of Britain from the Continent, before the location of the Belgæ in the island,—the unsettled and martial character of the various tribes occupying the country between the present Calais and its neighbourhood, and the mouths of the Rhone,—and add to these the fact, that Marseilles was not founded earlier than B.C. 600, and Narbo not until four hundred years later, it is presumed that none will be disposed to contend that tin was taken from Britain by this overland route, before that date, namely, B.C. 600. Can there be a vestige of probability in such a supposition? That the Phœnicians could have any part in it, is simply absurd. If they conducted the commerce in Cornwall, it would be infinitely more to their advantage to take the commodity direct in their vessels to Cadiz, than to transport it to Gaul, allow it to go entirely out of their hands for a thirty days' land journey, and then to re-ship it at the mouth of the Rhone. This could not have been the case. Yet, prior to this date, the trade had attained its widest extent.

About the year B.C. 600, or near the time that Marseilles was founded, Ezekiel speaks of the commerce of Tyre, and names tin procured from Tarshish as one of the principal commodities sold in their "fairs." Whence was this obtained, and by what route did it reach Tyre? All our researches have conducted us to the conclusion, that the principal part of this tin was found in Britain, and brought from thence, in Phœnician vessels, by the way of Gades to Tyre. We have to the best of our ability honestly dealt with every objection, and have only been led to adhere more strongly to the opinions on this subject, which we published long since, and which we have always entertained.

It now becomes our duty to place before the reader the positive information which ancient authors have recorded respecting this traffic. By this means he will be enabled to judge of the soundness of our conclusions, from data of acknowledged authority. These extracts will be given, as nearly as possible, in the order in which they were written, with an occasional observation when necessary.

Ezekiel, who prophesied about or soon after B.C. 600, in his brilliant catalogue of the traffic of Tyre, says, "Tarshish was thy merchant by reason of the multitude of all kinds of riches: with silver, iron, tin, and lead, they traded in thy fairs." *

* Ezekiel xxvii. 12.

Herodotus, the well-known father of Grecian history, who wrote B.C. 440, says, with reference to this subject:—" Of that part of Europe nearest to the west, I am not able to speak with decision. I by no means believe that the barbarians give the name of Eridanus to a river which empties itself into the Northern Sea; whence, it is said, our amber comes. Neither am I better acquainted with the islands called the Cassiterides, from which we are said to have our tin. The name Eridanus is certainly not barbarous; it is of Greek derivation, and, as I should conceive, introduced by one of our poets. I have endeavoured, but without success, to meet with some one who, from ocular observation, might describe to me the sea which lies in that part of Europe.* It is nevertheless certain that both our tin and our amber are brought from those extreme regions." †

Julius Cæsar, about B.C. 40, made this

* Herodotus could not have alluded to the Italian Eridanus, or Po. There can be no doubt of the accuracy of Larcher's comment on the place: "The Eridanus, here alluded to, could not possibly be any other than the Rhodaune, which empties itself into the Vistula, near Dantzic; and on the banks of which amber is now found in large quantities."

† Thalia, cxv.

statement: "The inland parts of Britain are inhabited by those, whom fame reports to be the natives of the soil. The sea-coast is peopled with the Belgians, drawn thither by the love of war and plunder. These last, passing over from different parts, and settling in the country, still retain the names of the several states whence they are descended. The island is well peopled, full of houses, built after the manner of the Gauls, and abounds in cattle. They use brass money, and iron rings of a certain weight. The provinces remote from the sea produce tin; and those upon the coast, iron; but the latter in no great quantity. Their brass is all imported. All kinds of wood grow here the same as in Gaul, except the fir and beech-tree. They think it unlawful to feed upon hares, pullets, or geese; yet they breed them up for their diversion and pleasure. The climate is more temperate than in Gaul, and the cold less intense. The island is triangular, one of its sides facing Gaul. The extremity towards Kent, whence is the nearest passage to Gaul, lies eastward; the other stretches south-west. This side extends about five hundred miles. Another side looks toward Spain, westward. Over against this lies Ireland, an island esteemed not above half as large as Britain, and separated from it by an interval equal to that between Britain and Gaul. In this interval lies the isle of Mona, besides several other lesser islands, of which some write, that in the time of the winter solstice they have night for thirty days together. We could make out nothing of this upon inquiry; only discovered by means of our hour glasses, that the nights were shorter than in Gaul. The length of this side is computed at seven hundred miles. The last side faces the north-east, and is fronted by no part of the Continent, only towards one of its extremities it seems to eye chiefly the German coast. It is thought to extend in length about eight hundred miles.......The inhabitants of Kent, which lies wholly on the sea-coast, are the most civilized of all the Britons, and differ but little in their manner from the Gauls. The greater part of those within the country never sow their lands, but live on flesh and milk, and go clad in skins. All the Britons in general paint themselves with woad, which gives a bluish cast to the skin, and makes them look dreadful in battle." *

Diodorus the Sicilian wrote just before our era, B.C. 8. He has given the following account

* "Wars," v., 12.

of the Phœnician trade and the traffic with Britain for tin:—" The Phœnicians in ancient times undertook frequent voyages by sea, in the way of traffic as merchants, so that they planted many colonies both in Africa and in these western parts of Europe. These merchants, succeeding in their undertaking, and thereupon growing very rich, passed at length beyond the Pillars of Hercules, into the sea called the Ocean; and first they built a city called Gades, near to the Pillars of Hercules, at the sea-side, in an isthmus in Europe; in which, among other things proper for the place, they built a stately temple to Hercules, and instituted splendid sacrifices to be offered to him after the rites and customs of the Phœnicians. This temple is in great veneration at this day, as well as in former ages; so that many of the Romans, famous and renowned both for their births and glorious actions, have made their vows to this god, and, after success in their affairs, have faithfully performed them. The Phœnicians, therefore, upon the account before related, having found out the coasts beyond the Pillars, and sailing along by the shore of Africa, were on a sudden driven by a furious storm afar off into the main ocean; and after they had lain under this violent tempest for many days, they at length arrived at this island; and so coming to the nature and pleasantness of this isle, they were the first that discovered it to others.

"Over against the French shore, opposite to the Hercynian Mountains, which are the greatest of any in Europe, there lie in the ocean many islands; the greatest of which is that which they call Britain, which anciently remained untouched, free from all foreign force; for it was never known that either Bacchus, Hercules, or any of the ancient heroes or princes, ever made any attempt upon it by force of arms; but Julius Cæsar in our time (who by his great achievements gained the title of 'Divine') was the first that conquered the island, and compelled the Britons to pay tribute. But these things shall be more particularly treated of in the proper time. We shall now only say something concerning the island, and the tin that is found there.

"In form it is triangular, like Sicily; but the sides are unequal. It lies in an oblique line, over against the continent of Europe; so that the promontory called Cantium,* next to the continent, is, they say, about a hundred fur-

* Kent.

longs from the land. Here the sea ebbs and flows. But the other point, Balerium,* is four days' sail from the continent.

"The last, called Horcas, or Oreas,† runs out far into the sea. The least of the sides facing the whole continent is seven thousand and five hundred furlongs in length; the second, stretching out itself all along from the sea to the highest point, is fifteen thousand furlongs; and the last is twenty thousand;—so that the whole compass of the island is forty-two thousand five hundred furlongs. The inhabitants are the original people thereof, and live to this present time after their own ancient manner and custom. In fights they use chariots, as it is said the old Grecian heroes did in the Trojan War. They dwell in mean cottages, covered for the most part with reeds or sticks. In reaping their corn, they cut off the ears from the stalk, and so house them up in repositories under ground; from thence they take them and pluck out the grains of as many of the oldest as may serve them for the day; and, after they have bruised the corn, make it into bread. They are of much sincerity and integrity, far from the craft and knavery of men among us, contented with

---

* The Land's End.   † The extreme north of Scotland.

plain and homely fare, strangers to the excess and luxury of rich men. The island is very populous, but of a cold climate, subject to frosts, being under the Arctic pole.* They are governed by several kings and princes, who for the most part are at peace and amity with each other. But of their laws, and other things peculiar to this island, we shall treat more particularly when we come to Cæsar's expedition into Britain.

"Now we shall speak something concerning the tin that is dug and gotten there. They that inhabit the British promontory of Balerium, by reason of their converse with merchants, are more civilized and courteous to strangers than the rest are. These are the people that make the tin, which, with a great deal of care and labour, they dig out of the ground; and that being rocky, the metal is mixed with some veins of earth, out of which they melt the metal, and then refine it; then they beat it into four square pieces like a die, and carry it to a British isle near at hand, called Ictis; for at low tide, all being dry between them and the island, they convey over in carts abundance of tin in the mean time. But there is one thing peculiar to those

* The constellation of the Bear.

islands, which lie between Britain and Europe; for at full sea they appear to be islands, but at low water for a long way they look like so many peninsulas. Hence the merchants transport the tin they buy of the inhabitants to France; and for thirty days' journey they carry it in packs on horses' backs through France to the mouth of the river Rhone. Thus much concerning tin."
"Above Lusitania there is much of this tin metal, that is, in the islands lying in the ocean over against Iberia, which are therefore called Cassiterides; and much of it likewise is transported out of Britain into Gaul, the opposite continent, which the merchants carry on horseback through the heart of Celtica, to Marseilles, and the city called Narbo." *

Strabo, about A.D. 18, wrote on this subject:—"The Cassiterides are ten in number, and lie near each other in the ocean toward the north from the haven of the Artabri. One of them is desert, but the others are inhabited by men in black cloaks, clad in tunics reaching to the feet, girt about the breast, and walking with staves, thus resembling the furies we see in tragic representations. They subsist by their cattle, leading for the most

* DIODORUS SICULUS, v., 2.

part a wandering life.* Of the metals, they have tin and lead, which, with skins, they barter with the merchants for earthenware, salt, and brasen vessels. Formerly, the Phœnicians alone carried on this traffic from Gades, concealing the passage from every one; and when the Romans followed a certain ship-master, that they also might find the market, the ship-master of jealousy purposely ran his vessel upon a shoal, leading on those who followed him into the same destructive disaster; he himself escaped by means of a fragment of the ship, and received from the state the value of the cargo he had lost. The Romans, nevertheless, by frequent efforts discovered the passage; and as soon as Publius Crassus, passing over to them, perceived that the metals were dug out at a little depth, and

---

* This brings to recollection the account of Tacitus:— "Women were seen rushing through the ranks in wild disorder, their apparel funereal, their hair loose in the wind, in their hands flaming torches, and their whole appearance resembling the frantic rage of furies. The Druids were ranged in order, with hands uplifted, invoking the gods and pouring forth horrible imprecations. The novelty of the sight struck the Romans with awe and terror. They stood in stupid amazement, as if their limbs were benumbed, riveted to one spot, a mark for the enemy."—"Annals," xiv., 30.

that the men were peaceably disposed, he declared it to those who already wished to traffic in this sea for profit, although the passage was longer than that to Britain.* Thus far concerning Iberia and the adjacent islands." †

Pliny, who wrote about A.D. 79, has scattered throughout his "Natural History" several notices of Gades, tin, and the countries whence it is procured. He says, speaking of England, "Opposite to this coast is the island called Britannia, so celebrated in the records of Greece and of our own country;" then, having mentioned Hibernia, he says, "Of the remaining islands, none is said to have a greater circumference than one hundred and twenty-five miles. Among these there are the Orcades, forty in number, and situate within a short distance of each other, the seven islands called Acmodæ, the Hæbrides, thirty in number, and, between Hibernia and Britannia, the islands of Mona, Monapia, Ricina, Vectis, Limnus, and Andros. Below it are the islands called Samnis and Axantos; and opposite, scattered in the Ger-

---

* Viz., that the Cassiterides are farther removed from the coasts of Spain than the rest of the southern coasts of Britain.

† STRABO, iii., v., 11.

man Sea, are those known as the Glæssariæ, but which the Greeks have more recently called the Electrides, from the circumstance of their producing *electrum*, or amber. The most remote of all that we find mentioned is Thule, in which, as we have previously stated, there is no night at the summer solstice, when the sun is passing through the sign of Cancer; while, on the other hand, at the winter solstice there is no day. Some writers are of opinion that this state of things lasts for six whole months together. Timæus, the historian, says, that an island called Mictis is within six days' sail of Britannia, in which white lead is found; and that the Britons sail over to it in boats of osier covered with sewed hides. There are writers, also, who make mention of some other islands,—Scandia, namely, Dumna, Bergos, and, greater than all, Nerigos, from which persons embark for Thule. At one day's sail from Thule is the Frozen Ocean, which by some is called the Cronian Sea." *

Writing of the "Islands in the Ocean," the same author says, "Opposite to Celtiberia are a number of islands, by the Greeks called Cassiterides, in consequence of their

* Pliny's "Natural History," book iv., chap. 30 (16).

abounding in tin; and, facing the promontory of the Arrotrebæ, are the six islands of the gods, which some persons have called the Fortunate Islands. At the very commencement of Bætica, and twenty-five miles from the mouths of the Straits of Gades, is the island of Gadis, twelve miles long and three broad, as Polybius states in his writings. At its nearest part, it is less than seven hundred feet distant from the mainland, while in the remaining portion it is distant more than seven miles. Its circuit is fifteen miles, and it has on it a city which enjoys the rights of Roman citizens, and whose people are called the Augustani of the City of Julia Gaditana. On the side which looks towards Spain, at about one hundred paces' distance, is another long island, three miles wide, on which the original city of Gades stood. By Ephorus and Philistides it is called Erythia, by Timæus and Silenus Aphrodisias, and by the natives the Isle of Juno. Timæus says, that the larger island used to be called Cotinusa, from its olives; the Romans call it Tartessos; the Carthaginians, Gadir,—that word in the Punic language signifying 'a hedge.' It was called Erythia because the Tyrians, the original ancestors of the Carthaginians, were said to have come from the Erythræan or Red Sea. In this island Geryon is by some thought to have dwelt, whose herds were carried off by Hercules. Other persons, again, think that his island is another one, opposite to Lusitania, and that it was there formerly called by that name."*

Further on in his treatise, when writing of lead mines and of white and black lead, Pliny says, "The nature of lead comes next to be considered. There are two kinds of it, the white and the black. The white is the most valuable: it was called by the Greeks *cassiteros;* and there is a fabulous story told of their going in quest of it to the islands of the Atlantic, and of its being brought in barks made of osiers, and covered with hides. It is now known that it is the production of Lusitania and Gallæcia. It is a sand found on the surface of the earth, and of a black colour, and is only to be detected by its weight. It is mingled with small pebbles, particularly in the dried beds of rivers. The miners wash this sand, and calcine the deposit in the furnace. It is also found in the gold mines that are known as *alutiæ*, the stream of water which is passed through them detaching cer-

* PLINY's "Natural History," book iv., chap. 36.

tain black pebbles, mottled with small white spots, and of the same weight as gold. Hence it is that they remain with the gold in the baskets in which it is collected; and, being separated in the furnace, are then melted, and become converted into white lead.

"Black lead is not procured in Gallæcia, although it is so greatly abundant in the neighbouring province of Cantabria; nor is silver procured from white lead, although it is from black. Pieces of black lead cannot be soldered without the intervention of white lead, nor can this be done without employing oil; nor can white lead, on the other hand, be united without the aid of black lead. White lead was held in estimation in the days even of the Trojan War,—a fact that is attested by Homer, who calls it 'cassiteros.' There are two different sources of black lead: it being procured either from its own native ore, where it is produced without the intermixture of any other substance, or else from an ore which contains it in common with silver, the two metals being fused together. The metal which first becomes liquid in the furnace is called *stannum*; the next that melts is silver; and the metal that remains behind is galena,—the third constituent part of the mineral. On this last being again submitted to fusion, black lead is produced, with a deduction of two-ninths." *

"India has neither copper nor lead; but she procures them in exchange for her precious stones and pearls." †

"Black lead is used in the form of pipes and sheets. It is extracted with great labour in Spain, and throughout all the Gallic provinces; but in Britannia it is found in the upper stratum of the earth in such abundance, that a law has been spontaneously made, prohibiting any one from working more than a certain quantity of it." ‡

It will be desirable, before proceeding further, to make some observations on these several statements, with a view to ascertain their respective meaning, and, as far as it may be possible, to harmonize their teaching, without doing violence to the text of the ancient writers.

From the entire account given by Ezekiel, (xxvii.,) it is very plain that Tyre was at the time he wrote in the zenith of her commercial splendour, and was the grand emporium for the merchandise of the world. A range of traffic which extended from Spain to Arabia,

* PLINY's "Natural History," book xxxiv., chap. 47 (16).
† *Ibid.*, chap. 48 (17). ‡ *Ibid.*, chap. 49.

and included every place of importance in the then known world, must have required centuries to rear up, and fully confirms the very early date which is given to the rise of the Phœnician people as a great commercial power. The trade in tin is attributed to Tarshish, as "the merchant" for the commodity, without any mention of the place whence it was procured.

Herodotus speaks with great caution on this subject. "Still, taking the text of his statement as it stands, the real fact it embodies is, that the tin country of Western Europe was known to him;"* although not so minutely and fully as he desired. This is what might be expected, considering the age in which he wrote, and the jealous care with which the Phœnicians kept secret the seats of their most distant and profitable commercial operations. It was not likely that he could obtain very full information respecting the Cassiterides. But this comparative ignorance of the father of history is strong evidence that the tin trade had not yet been diverted from the maritime course to the overland route through Gaul to Marseilles. If in his day the Phocean Greeks of that city

* Dr. William Smith's "Dictionary of Geography," vol. i., p. 432.

were the tin merchants for the East, it could scarcely have escaped his notice; and if he knew this, he would have had the means of learning all he wished respecting the place whence the commodity was procured. The testimony of Herodotus is, however, clear and decisive. Although he avows that his information was limited as to the situation of the Cassiterides, and of the country in the North whence amber was reported to have been brought, he was not, like more modern writers, ready to denounce as fiction or fable any report or tradition respecting which he could not obtain clear and sufficient information. Herodotus did what he could,—he inquired into the circumstances of this trade; and although he could not be fully satisfied respecting the geography of the Cassiterides, or of the river whence amber was procured, he had convinced himself that no other country produced these commodities. He accordingly records the positive assertion, "It is nevertheless certain, that both our tin and our amber are brought from these extreme regions." *

* The geographical knowledge of the Greeks, for a century after Herodotus,—and which, like his, must chiefly have been obtained from Phœnician sources,—may be seen

The account given by Cæsar appears to be decisive against the notion, that the overland route for tin to Marseilles had been opened before his day. If it had existed, he must have known of it. Having conquered Gaul, and convened the merchants trading with Britain for the special purpose of procuring information concerning the island, this fact could not have been concealed, had the trade existed at that time. It must also be remembered that Cæsar did not collect his information at Rome, but at Boulogne, Calais, and Dover, where any overland traffic with Britain must have been a subject of notoriety. The only remark made by the Roman chief on this subject is, "The provinces remote from the sea produce tin," —words which prove his knowledge that the metal was found in the island; and his igno-

---

in the following passage from Aristotle: "Beyond the Pillars of Hercules, the ocean flows round the earth: in this ocean, however, are two islands, and those very large, called Britannia, Albion and Ierne, which are larger than those before mentioned, and lie beyond the Kelti; and other two not less than these, Taprobane, beyond the Indians, lying obliquely in respect of the main land, and that called Phebol, situate over against the Arabic Gulf: moreover, not a few small islands, around the Britannic Isles and Iberia, encircle as with a diadem this earth, which we have already said to be an island." (*De Mundo*, c. 3.)

rance of the locality whence it was brought, and of all the circumstances of the trade. For, although the part of Britain where tin was found, was remote from the only sea-coast of the island with which he was acquainted, it was, nevertheless, also on the sea-coast. And as he specially mentions other branches of merchandise, and does not say a word respecting the tin trade, the fair presumption is that he knew nothing of it. But he must have known it had it been carried on overland to Marseilles.

From the account of Diodorus, it seems evident, that, during the half century which elapsed from the time of Cæsar to that of the Sicilian author, British tin had been transferred across Gaul to the mouth of the Rhone. Tyre had fallen, and Carthage had perished; Gades had been independent for a while, but at this time all Spain had been for a long period a Roman province. The conditions of the tin trade had entirely changed. The mild sway of Augustus had given peace to the whole Roman empire; and there was now no reason why the Gallic citizens of Rome might not extend their trade to the extreme southwest of the British island, take tin, with other commodities, to Boulogne or any other French port, and send it overland to Marseilles.

There never was a greater error in commercial geography than that committed by the learned Whitaker, and those who have followed him, in supposing that the Isle of Wight is the Ictis of Diodorus. It assumes that, nineteen hundred years ago, this island was near the mainland, and separated from it by a channel so shallow as to be dry at low water, when carts could easily pass over with merchandise,—an assumption in itself most improbable, and unsupported by a tittle of physical evidence. And this very strange supposition is based on the fact, that its ancient name, Vectes, identifies it with the Ictis of Diodorus, notwithstanding the essential difference between the two names, and the improbability that one would merge into the other. And for what purpose are these daring suppositions assumed as facts? For the purpose of challenging belief in a statement more incredible than was ever before propounded by sober men, namely, that tin was taken by land two hundred miles, to be shipped at the Isle of Wight, when there were harbours equally good close to the localities where the metal was raised! And this is assumed as the means of harmonizing the facts with the statement of an author who distinctly says, that the men who dig and prepare the tin carry it "to a British isle *near at hand*," but which, according to this notion, was two hundred miles off. The Gallic or Roman vessels which came from France to the Isle of Wight, could with equal ease have extended their voyage to the excellent harbour of Falmouth, well known to the Romans, or to Mount's Bay. The Ictis of Diodorus is undoubtedly St. Michael's Mount, in the bay above-mentioned, and to which it gives its name.

We have anticipated our comment on the statement of Strabo, by showing, on a preceding page, that the coast of Cornwall is opposite to, or, as this author correctly says, "north from, the haven of the Artabri," or the modern Corunna. This in itself is sufficient to identify Cornwall with the Cassiterides of this geographer. We have then to call attention to his positive assertion, that "formerly the Phœnicians alone carried on this traffic from Gades." This testimony is most important, and will have due weight with every considerate mind. Nor is there anything in the story of the Phœnician captain luring the Roman vessel to destruction, rather than allow it to track the way to the Tin Islands, which might not in such an age have occurred. But, if it happened, it must have been subsequent to the fall of Tyre, and probably during the rivalry of Carthage and Rome. The discovery of the Tin Islands by Publius Crassus must, if the conjecture of Sir G. Cornewall Lewis concerning him is correct, have taken place after the time of Julius Cæsar.*

The first sentence we have quoted from Pliny gives no countenance to the notion that Britain was a country unknown to the Greeks and Romans. He speaks of it as "celebrated in the records of Greece and of our own (the Roman) country." It is very difficult to reconcile the geography of this author to the names and localities known to us. The Oreades have been supposed to be the Orkneys, the Acmodæ the islands of Shetland; some of the other names have been referred to parts of the coast of Norway; but in respect of all these, various opinions have

* In explanation of the concluding sentence of the passage quoted from Strabo, that the passage to the Cassiterides was farther from the coast of Europe than that to Britain, it may be observed, that Strabo evidently fell into the common error of his day, and believed the tin districts of Cornwall to be islands, and not a part of Britain.

obtained among the learned. But the grand point on which the utmost difference of opinion has been entertained is the locality of Thule. No less than seven or eight different places have been supposed to have borne this name. It is sufficiently evident, that no island in those seas answers all the conditions of Pliny's description. Indeed, his description is evidently greatly exaggerated; and, happily, we are not called on to pronounce judgment on the conflicting opinions which have been formed on the subject. Much the same may be said respecting the supposed island, *Mictis*. No island which produces tin lies within six days' sail of Britain. In all these cases the geography of Pliny is more or less at fault. He had been in Belgic Gaul, and held, under Nero, the office of Procurator in Spain; he was, therefore, well acquainted with the western coast of Europe; but he does not appear to have had any accurate knowledge of Britain, or of its neighbouring islands. It is by no means improbable that the conjecture of Brotier is correct, namely, that by *Mictis* he meant Cornwall, which was erroneously supposed to be an island, and which, when the vessels he describes were used, might have been six days' sail from that part of Britain with which he was acquainted. Pliny, with his defective information, might well esteem it a fable, that all the tin was brought from Mictis; but it is nevertheless, as his learned annotator observes, "not very remote from the truth. The ores of tin are known to exist in Gallicia; but the mines in that country are scanty compared to those of Cornwall." * It is, indeed, a well-attested fact, that the Cassiterides supplied the ancient world with tin, as the same neighbourhood still continues to furnish the greater part of such supplies. There is considerable probability that the account which Pliny gives of the finding of stones of tin ores in the beds of brooks, and on the surface of the ground, is correct. The tin veins reaching the surface were exposed to all the changes of the atmosphere, the action of rain and rivulets from the hills; stones of tin and gravel, with sand containing tin, were thus washed down into the valleys, and found as described.

The testimony of this Roman writer to the antiquity of this trade, and his statements that tin was in use and highly esteemed before the time of the Trojan war, is in harmony with all the other accounts which have been

* Bostock's note, Pliny's "Natural History," Bohn's edition, vol. vi., p. 212.

quoted. His positive assertion that in his day tin was not produced in India, although so highly esteemed there that precious stones and pearls were given in exchange for this metal, should not be forgotten, especially by those who have been inclined to look to the East for supplies of the article in ancient times.

We are now prepared to furnish a sketch of the rise and progress of this branch of ancient commerce, as far as the fragments of information which have come down to us will permit.

The Phœnician territory in Palestine, the home and seat of the nation, was very limited in extent. It was a part of the Syrian coast, extending from Tyre to Aradus, about a hundred and twenty miles in length, and averaging about twenty in width. It was favoured with many excellent bays and harbours, and numerous islands studded the coast, while the land was divided by lofty mountains. Sidon, the parent city of the state, was founded in times so remote, that no record or legend affords any information respecting it; nor is it possible to fix with certainty the date of Tyre. Herodotus says, that the Tyrians boasted to him that their temple and city had been built 2,300 years before his time; and great weight is due to his authority. But Dr. Hales, regarding this statement as an exaggeration, fixed the foundation of the city at B.C. 2267; believing that the "numeral letter denoting a thousand was dropped from the text of Josephus." * This is not a very satisfactory reason, although it derives some probability from the fact that Josephus had the best means of information on the subject, and his date, 1267 B.C., is notoriously incorrect. For Joshua, about B.C. 1600, repeatedly calls the parent city "the great Zidon;" † and speaks of the more recent capital as "the strong city of Tyre." ‡

The extreme antiquity of Sidon is therefore undoubted, and her commerce and manufactures gave her early and universal celebrity. Jacob, who was in Palestine about B.C. 1900, alludes to the practice of navigation by this people: "Zebulon shall dwell at the haven of the sea, and he shall be for an haven of ships; and his border shall be unto Zidon." § Herodotus confirms the early devotion of this people to maritime pursuits, by asserting that from their earliest occupation of the country,

* "Chronology," vol. i., p. 444.   † Joshua xi. 8; xix. 28.
‡ Joshua xix. 29.   § Genesis xlix. 13.

they "soon distinguished themselves by their long and enterprising voyages."* Justin asserts, that Tyre was founded a year before the fall of Troy. Having mentioned the building of Sidon, he says, "Many years after, their city being stormed by the king of the Ascalonians, sailing away to the place where Tyre stands, they built that city the year before the fall of Troy."† But it is certain, from what is stated above, that this city existed some centuries before this time, so that Justin could not mean the first erection of Tyre. This is apparent from his own account. The word he uses to set forth this building of the city, is precisely the same as he employs to describe the restoration of it by Alexander. It is probable, therefore, that Tyre, having existed for a long time as inferior to Sidon, and a mart for its commerce, was, on the siege of the parent city, on account of its previous position and military strength, regarded as a suitable seat for the centre and metropolis of the people, and a refuge for the population of Sidon. So that when they found themselves unable to resist the king of Ascalon, they retired on board their ships with their families and property, and sailed to Tyre:

* Clio, 1. † xviii., 3.

which city henceforth became the Phœnician capital, and rapidly increased in wealth and population.

Afterward, in the days of their highest prosperity, the people of Tyre claimed for their city the honour of being the metropolis in the fullest sense, and even went so far as to place on a coin of the age of Antiochus IV., " Mother of the Sidonians." * But no claims of this kind can rebut the uniform testimony of all ancient history and tradition, that Sidon was, for many ages, the principal city of the Phœnician people. The early prosperity of Sidon, and the flourishing state of its commerce and manufactures, are attested by all the remains of antiquity which refer to the inhabitants of the coasts of the inner Mediterranean in ancient times. " The vase of silver which Achilles proposes as a prize in the funeral games in honour of Patroclus was a work of the 'skilful Sidonians.' The garment offered by Hecuba as a propitiation to Minerva was the work of the Sidonian women, whom Paris had brought with him to Troy, when he visited Phœnicia. The bowl of silver with edges of gold which Menelaus gives to Telemachus is called a work of Hephæston, and

* KENRICK's "Phœnicia," p. 58.

was given to him by a king of the Sidonians. The narrative of Eumæus exhibits Phœnicians at once as merchants and pirates. Sidon is spoken of in the same passage as abounding in works of brass. Ulysses also represents himself as having been left on the island of Ithaka by the Phœnicians while they sailed away to 'the well-peopled Sidonia.'" * To this enumeration we might add the breastplate of elaborate workmanship presented by the king of Cyprus to Agamemnon, as already mentioned, and many other curious and costly works noticed incidentally by ancient authors;† but these are sufficient to show that in the earliest ages, before Tyre had arisen into prominence and honour, the Phœnicians were famous for their navigation, manufactures, and commerce. It will be universally admitted that these must have attained a high degree of perfection to have earned such great celebrity. Without extensive navigation and commerce, materials for these manufactures could not possibly have been obtained in that age. This people were the first in the field; they had to create a navy, to

---

* Kenrick's "Phœnicia," p. 341.

† See Homer's "Iliad," vi., 290; xxiii., 743, 744; "Odyssey," xv., 415-484.

found colonies, to search out the countries where the various necessary productions could be procured; and then to acquire all the arts employed in the manufacture of a vast range of articles of unrivalled excellence and value.

In order that the thorough commercial character of this people may be appreciated, it is necessary to observe that their devotion to trade appears to have excluded all ideas of political aggrandizement, and almost of national unity. An eminent author gives the following account of this country: "The sea, which broke with great fury upon this rocky shore, had probably separated some of these promontories from the mainland, and which, forming little islands at a small distance from the shore, are not less worthy of note than the mainland itself, being everywhere covered with extensive colonies and flourishing cities. Thus, Aradus, the most northern frontier city of Phœnicia, was built on one of these islands; and opposite to it on the mainland was Antaradus, which derived its name from it. About eighteen miles from the south of this stood, and still stands, Tripolis; and at a like distance, Byblus, with the temple of Adonis; and again, further south, Berytus. Keeping along the coast, we come to Sidon at nearly the same distance; and, finally, fourteen or fifteen miles further, at the extreme southern boundary of the country, was erected upon another island the stately Tyre, the queen of Phœnician cities. The space between those places was covered with a number of towns of less import, but equally the abode of industry, and widely celebrated for their arts and manufactures. Among these were Serephta, Botrys, Orthosia, and others, forming one unbroken city, extending along the whole line of coast and over the islands; and which, with the harbours and sea-ports, and the numerous fleets lying within them, must have afforded altogether a spectacle scarcely to be excelled in the world, and must have excited in the stranger who visited them the highest idea of the opulence, the power, and the enterprising spirit of the inhabitants."[*] Such was ancient Phœnicia.

But the extraordinary result of that spirit of which we have spoken, is, as already said, the absence, as far as we can learn, of all attempts to establish and maintain a political and military unity among this remarkable people. We never hear of a king of Phœnicia, nor of a

[*] Heeren's "Historical Researches, Asiatic Nations," vol. ii., p. 9.

Phœnician army. The country never became one state. Each of the principal cities, Sidon, Tyre, Aradus, and Byblus, had its own king, who ruled over it and an adjoining territory. It was the same with the Phœnician colonies. Cyprus had its own king before the Trojan war. There were undoubtedly times when all these would feel that their interests required a union of all their powers to maintain the common safety; but this would be an alliance of sovereign states, and not the action of one people. In the time of the greatest power of Tyre, there can be no doubt that she exercised a dominant influence over the smaller cities; but it was their subjection, not their allegiance, that was secured. If the power of Persia prevailed, the accustomed tribute would be transferred from Tyre to it, as a necessary result. The same peculiarity is seen in respect of their military power. Although in their early history it is well known that the Phœnicians were pirates as well as merchants, and made provision in their voyages, not only for their own defence, but also for aggressive measures, when these would serve their purpose; yet they do not appear to have formed any large native military force, but rather to have relied on contingents supplied by their colonies, and on other hired troops, even for the defence of their royal cities. Hence the Hebrew prophet says, "They of Persia, of Lydia, and of Lycia, were thy warriors: they hanged their shields and helmets in thee. They of Arvad were in thine army, about thy walls, and kept watch before thy gates: they hanged their shields upon thy towers, and have thus made thee illustrious."*

But, as the father of history has said, "the long and enterprising voyages" which were prosecuted by this people, soon after their settlement in Palestine, laid the foundation of this wide-spread greatness. Their soil neither in quantity nor quality was calculated to produce great wealth; while their genius and inclination led them to maritime pursuits. As we have already shown, the neighbouring islands were first colonized, and their mineral and vegetable productions carefully collected and applied to the purposes of manufacture and commerce. It is highly probable, that most of the isles of the Grecian Archipelago were occupied and explored for these purposes, and several were afterward abandoned as not being sufficiently valuable; and others to avoid war, when the Carians, and subsequently

* Ezekiel xxvii. 10, 11.

the Greeks, extended their colonies to those islands, and even to Asia Minor. But discouragements of this kind did not check the ardour of this indomitable people. What they lost in the north-east, was amply compensated by a great extension in the west. We have already noticed the great extent of their colonization in Crete, Sicily, Malta, Sardinia, the continent of Africa, and even to the Atlantic coasts of Spain.

But although indisputable evidence can be given in proof of this vast range of early Phœnician navigation, we are well aware, that men still look doubtingly on the subject, and say that this wide extent of maritime and commercial enterprise, at such an early date, must have required the greatest courage and genius of the most skilful navigator that ever ploughed the ocean; and more than can reasonably be expected to have been called into operation at this early period of the world's history. And the reasonable objection has been urged,—If such an effort had been successfully made; if the wild Atlantic had been explored, and the mineral treasures of Spain and Britain had been discovered and realized; surely we might fairly expect to hear something at least of the daring individual by whom these great deeds were achieved,—of the man who, by these discoveries, threw open the treasures of the western world, for the aggrandizement of the east. We have called this a reasonable expectation; and in ordinary circumstances, and within the historical period of this world's action, it would be perfectly reasonable. But where are we to look for the recorded accounts of these discoveries? The annals of Sidon and Tyre have perished. These events transpired before Grecian history began: where then shall we seek for their memorials?

In order to obtain any light on this subject, even though it be to a limited extent, we must remember, that the events of which we speak took place at a period in which every notable action or eminent personage in Gentile lands became prominent in religious myth, or mythological legends. High esteem, and a grateful appreciation of noble deeds, at this period, almost always merged ultimately into idolatrous veneration. It is nevertheless more than probable, that usually there were many intermediate steps which we are prone to overlook. At first images, or, as we should say, statues, would be raised to testify an acknowledgment of the worth of the eminent living, or the illustrious dead: these, placed among the statues of their deities, were by the people at no distant day regarded as Divine.

Guided by these general principles, if we look into the Pantheon of Tyre, we find their principal deity called Hercules. But abundant evidence proves that the accounts given of this deity were altogether different from those current of the Grecian Hercules; although there can be no question but that many of the exploits of the celebrated Tyrian have been incorporated into the labours of the deified Greek. The Tyrian hero is frequently spoken of as a native of Egypt,* and was worshipped † long before the son of Alcmene was born. Herodotus was so much interested and puzzled by what he heard in Egypt on this subject, that, unable to obtain a satisfactory solution of his doubts in that country, he made a voyage to Tyre, expressly for the purpose of getting the desired information.‡ He there learned from the priests, that the Tyrian Hercules was adored in Phœnicia before he was known in Greece. With this truth before us, we direct attention to the fact, that

* Tacitus's "Annals," ii., 160.
† Herodotus, Euterpe, 47. ‡ *Ibid.*, 44, 45.

the noble exploits in navigation and discovery which were necessary to lay open the western world, are so similar to the fabulous account of the tenth labour of the Grecian Hercules, that we are irresistibly brought to the conclusion, that the daring and successful prowess of the great Tyrian led to the conception of the elaborate legends which, in this portion of his toils, adorn the character of the son of Jupiter. It will be recollected that the scene of the Greek hero commenced in the Mediterranean sea, and extended to Africa, whence he journeyed westward to the straits known by his name, where he is said to have erected a pillar on each promontory. He then prosecuted his expedition to Iberia, "to make war upon the son of Chrysaor, the rich-in-gold," where his exploits were so great and successful that he secured the spoils and treasures which he sought.

This application of the Greek legend is not a fancy of ours. The similarity is so evident that it has forced itself on the notice of the most eminent authors who have treated on the subject. Heeren, alluding to this similarity, observes, "The attempt to clear up and explain every particular of this fable would be doing violence to the manes of remote antiquity. Some of the principal features of this allegory I shall nevertheless venture to expose, fearless of incurring this reproach.

"Hercules is said to have undertaken his expedition with a numerous fleet, which assembled at Crete; an island forming, as will presently be seen, one of the principal links of the Phœnician chain of colonies. Its object was Spain, the country abounding in gold, and where Chrysaor, the father of Geryon, reigned. Hercules passed through Africa, where he introduced agriculture, and built the great city Hecatompylos. He thus came to the strait, which he crossed over to Gades. Spain submitted to him, and he carried away the oxen of Geryon as booty; taking his way back through Gaul, Italy, and the isles of Sicily and Sardinia.

"The principal features of this allegory seem scarcely to require an explanation. It is only among a maritime people that this mythos could have been formed, as a fleet is fitted out for the undertaking. That this took place at Crete, the most convenient island, shows that the party did not extend their views beyond the western Mediterranean until they had well established their dominion over the eastern islands. Neither did they undertake these expeditions for the mere purpose of destruction and conquest. They carried civilization with them; they instructed the barbarians in the art of agriculture, and accustomed them to fixed dwellings. And where did this take place? Precisely in those countries which were colonized by the Phœnicians; that is, in Africa, Sicily, and Sardinia. But the express object of this expedition was, that very land which was the main source of Phœnician wealth, and the principal seat of its trade; namely, the southern and western parts of Spain. Thus the traditions, as they have been handed down to us by the poets, are in accordance with the historical facts. The Phœnicians gradually spread themselves round the coasts of the Mediterranean; they came at last to the Pillars of Hercules, and even went beyond them. But in every part their colonies were confined to the sea-coast; and hence it may fairly be concluded, that they owed their foundation to commerce." *

All who will carefully study this subject under the guidance of ancient authorities, will be led to the adoption of similar opinions. We accordingly find Mr. Kenrick, in his

* HEEREN'S "Researches, Asiatic Nations," vol. ii., p. 33.

most elaborate and convincing exposition of Phœnician history and commerce, conducting his readers to conclusions similar to those just quoted. He says:—"The gods whom we have hitherto mentioned belonged to Phœnicia generally. MELKARTH was the especial and tutelary god of Tyre, by the diffusion of whose colonies his worship was carried far and wide over the ancient world. His name, which denotes 'King of the City,' indicates this peculiar character. Under the slightly altered form of Melicertes, he appears in the Greek mythology, with the attributes of a maritime divinity, and the synonym of Palæmon, or 'the Wrestler,' an epithet of Hercules. The later Pagans considered Hercules as the sun, and the number of his twelve labours appears to have been fixed with an astronomical reference; but few, if any, of them have an astronomical origin. Those which relate to Egypt and Africa have evidently originated in the events of Phœnician colonization or commercial intercourse, considered from the Greek point of view, according to which Greece was the source and centre of all his undertakings, —the scene of his birth and his apotheosis. Wherever the Phœnicians had established his worship, there the Greeks supposed the Theban hero to have made an expedition, and performed some exploit, by which he proved himself superior to the native gods and heroes of the country. In Egypt he kills Busiris; from the gardens of the Hesperides he carries off the golden apples; under the name of Maceris he conquers Sardinia, at the head of a host of Libyans; he vanquishes Antæus, the guardian of the Libyan deserts; assumes the functions of Atlas in supporting the heavens; establishes his Pillars at the Straits; and drives off the herds of Geryones from Erytheia. In all these countries the Phœnicians had established themselves long before Greek mythology had been developed into form; and therefore we cannot hesitate in attributing these legends to the characteristic desire of the Greeks to appropriate everything to themselves. Nor is it unlikely that some of the labours of Hercules in Greece, in clearing the country, and exterminating wild beasts, may represent the influence of Phœnician civilization; or that his descent into Hades was suggested by the establishment of his worship in the extreme West, and on the verge of the unseen world." *

* KENRICK's "Phœnicia," p. 322.

Thus, either by deifying the hero who made these great discoveries, and opened up the shores of the Atlantic to the commerce of Phœnicia, or by identifying his actions with the attributes and character of the tutelary deity of Tyre, these exploits were celebrated by that people, and ultimately appropriated to adorn the mythological legends of Greece.

It is our object, as far as possible, to regard these various and curious legends as the permanent remains of measures taken at the period, in accordance with the usages of the times, to celebrate the great actions of this noble Phœnician discoverer. It will tend to show more fully the extent of these usages, in assigning the most important discoveries to this divinity, to state that the invention of letters was also ascribed to him,* as was the discovery of the Tyrian purple dye.† In the latter case, Hercules is represented as a philosopher, who saw a shepherd's dog with his mouth stained from biting the *concha*, and was thence led to the application of this dye to the colouring of cloths, which henceforth became an important article of commerce, and was

* Cicero *De Naturâ Deorum*, lib. iii., cap. 16.

† Palæphati *Fragmentum*, "*De Inventione Purpuræ*," ex *Fastis Siculis, sive Chronico Alexandrino*.

famed for its beauty throughout the world. But we have to confine ourselves more particularly to those myths which relate to the maritime and commercial discovery of this people, and to gather from the particular features of these legends, compared with the brief notices of the subject found in ancient authors, the real facts of this extensive commercial exploration and colonization. From these it appears that the Phœnicians, from their long-continued acquaintance with the Mediterranean coasts of France, ascertained that gold and silver mines were found in those countries,* and, despairing of securing any exclusive advantage in trade, with a people so martial in their habits as the ancient Gauls, determined to prosecute their researches farther to the south. In these efforts they found, at a short distance to the east of the Straits, the town and harbour of Malaca (Malaga). Here they effected a settlement, evidence of which remained in the Phœnician configuration of the place to the time of Strabo.† As gold was found in this neighbourhood, and it was less than one hundred miles overland to the country of Tartessus, which abounded in the precious metals, it is

* Strabo, lib. iv., cap. i., sec. 18.
† Lib. iii., cap. iv., sec. 2.

scarcely possible that a people so enterprising and inquisitive could have remained long ignorant of such an important fact. Does not this circumstance explain the account which Strabo has given in a religious form, and which appears on a preceding page? We are told, the expedition that was sent to form this colony, on offering the usual sacrifice, found the omens inauspicious, and returned for further instructions; that a second locality was tried with the same result, and that at length Gades was selected. Was this because, during their stay and inquiries at Malaga, they obtained information that a place nearer the great mineral field of the country might be secured, and one at the same time more remote from the intrusion of rival merchants? Did the same thing occur at Carteia? At Gades, however, they secured their object, and found themselves in the centre of the grand mineral field of Spain, and far away from the chance of competition. The dread of the great ocean was for ages the most potent bulwark that could possibly defend the new colony from intrusion or rivalry.

But although no particulars have reached us from this remote era, it is plain, from the legends and fables arising out of the subject, that the Phœnicians could not obtain peaceable possession of all they required, and that Melkarth had to enforce the object of his voyage by military power. It would seem that Geryon, the son of the king of Tartessus, opposed his progress in that country; and that, after a violent contest, the Tartessian prince was defeated and slain, and the conqueror rewarded with great spoil and undisputed possession of the territory. This Geryon is sometimes described as having had three heads, and at others three bodies. This fabulous representation has been explained as meaning that there were three brothers, sons * of the king, or that an alliance of three native princes, who acted in close concert, was formed for the expulsion of the strangers; but that they were quite subdued by the superior power of Melkarth and his forces.† Having put down all opposition, and obtained peaceful possession of the island on which Gades was afterward built, with as much of the country about Tartessus as he required, the Phœnician hero went northward, and took possession of the Cape Artabri, where he is said to have built

* Justin, xliv., 4.
† Banier's "Mythology," vol. iv., p. 88. Dionys. Hal., lib. i., c. 34 and 41. Diod. Sic., lib. iv., c. 1.

Corunna. A glance at the map of Europe will be sufficient to show the importance of a settlement at this place to any commercial people occupying Cadiz, and wishing to extend their trade to the more northern parts of Europe. The testimony of the ancient author is confirmed by a tradition still remaining, that at this place a tower was erected by the Phœnicians, and used as a pharos, and that it was dedicated to Hercules. This tower at a later period was repaired by the Romans and devoted to Mars. The tower still remains, and a Latin inscription on a metal plate affixed to it confirms the tradition; but a learned Spanish writer considers the present erection as a work of Trajan.*

Having placed his conquests in Spain under proper government, we are informed that the Phœnician hero proceeded northward through Celtica, (Gaul,) putting "an end to the usual impieties and murdering of strangers;" and then founded a city, which, on account of his

* MALTE-BRUN'S "Geography," vol. viii., p. 72. This eminent geographer considers it probable that the present name of the city was given on account of this ancient pharos. He says:—"It is not improbable that the word 'Corunna' has been derived from *Columna*; such, at least, was the name that the ancients gave a tower that was used as a pharos, in height and appearance not unlike a column."

long expedition, he called Alesia (Arras). This town was built on a hill in a very strong position, about fifty miles from the coast, and nearly midway between Boulogne and Dieppe. Whatever may be thought of the credibility of the Sicilian writer, there can be no mistake as to our clearly understanding him; for he says, that the barbarians who gathered to the place so greatly outnumbered the original citizens, that the latter soon learned their manners. He then adds, "The Celtæ at this day have a great esteem and honour for this city, as being the chief and metropolis of all Gaul; and ever since the time of Hercules it has remained free, and never been taken by any to our very days; till at length Caius Cæsar took it by storm, and so it came into the hands of the Romans."* Cæsar confirms the account of Diodorus as to the capture of this city, by informing us that it was the scene of the last stand made by Vercingetorix against the Romans, and that here this Gallic chief fell, with Alesia, into the power of the imperial conqueror.† But what will perhaps be regarded as most remarkable, is the fact that, in refer-

* Diod. Sic., lib. iv., cap. 1.
† Cæsar *De Bello Gallico*, book vii., chap. 79-89; Bryant's "Analysis of Ancient Mythology," vol. ii., p. 341.

ence to Alesia also, time-honoured reports confirm the statements of Diodorus. We are assured, "that, according to tradition, Alesia was founded by Hercules, which would imply that the place had been originally a Phœnician stronghold for purposes of inland traffic."* Nor is this the only evidence which identifies this town and district with Phœnician arts and influence. The people here were supposed to have invented the art of tinning articles of metal, and of plating with silver: they were at least distinguished for the very early practice of these arts. Pliny says:—"It was in the Gallic provinces that the method was discovered of coating articles of copper with white lead (tin), so as to be scarcely distinguishable from silver: articles thus plated are known as *incoctilia*.† At a later period the people of the town of Alesia began to use a similar process for plating articles with silver."‡ The account goes on to state, that after rearing this city, Hercules fought with the giants Albion and Bergion, and then passed through

* *De Bello Gallico*, book xvii., chap. 79, *note*. Bohn's edition.

† Literally, *inboiled*, being coated by immersion in molten tin.

‡ Pliny's "Natural History," book xxxiv., chap. 48 (17).

Gaul into Italy, where he waited for the return of his fleet. But we do not rely on these statements any further than they are confirmed by the planting of settlements, and sanctioned by prevalent traditions. If the Phœnician expedition prosecuted its voyage so extensively as these accounts evidently indicate, so as to be brought within sight of the cliffs of Britain, few will pronounce it improbable that they should have coasted its southern shores, so as to have discovered the part of the island where tin was abundantly produced. Further proofs of this may be given hereafter. But an observation may be made here, in explanation of the difficulty which has been supposed to arise from the statement that the Cassiterides were several islands, ten is the number sometimes given. It is not to be supposed that vessels sufficiently large to trade from Tyre to Gades, and then to navigate the Atlantic, would, in coasting the British shores, enter every bay and ascertain whether what appeared to be rivers were actually such, or branches of the sea dividing the country into islands. Such an expedition would more probably sail from cape to cape, as far, at least, as they could be seen, touching only at such places as they hoped would afford them information. In this way the western part of the country would appear as a number of islands, and be described as such. The author has now in his possession a large old folio atlas, which has California laid down as an island, from the cause just stated. The extent of the gulf had not been explored, and the peninsula joining it to the continent was accordingly unknown.

If our limits would allow, we might add further general support to the account already given of the reality and extent of Phœnician colonization; but our further citations must be very brief. Strabo, having alluded to several fictions of the poets, protests against the statement of the Phœnician colonization in the West being ranked with them. "I repeat," he says, "that the Phœnicians were the discoverers of those countries; for they possessed the better part of Iberia and Libya before the time of Homer, and continued masters of those places until their empire was overthrown by the Romans."* Speaking of the same countries, he says, "They fell so entirely under the dominion of the Phœnicians, that at the present day (A.D. 19) almost the whole of the cities of Turdetania and the neighbouring places are inhabited by them."† Justin

* Strabo, lib. iii., cap. 2. † *Ibid.*

also speaks of Tartessus and Gades as being subdued by Hercules, and brought under the power of the Phœnicians.*

Monumental remains, as well as legend and history, bear witness to the name of the Phœnician hero who discovered, or consolidated and extended, their colonization in the west. On the base of a marble candelabrum found in Malta, and which was a votive offering from two brothers to the Tyrian deity, there is an inscription in the Phœnician language, and also a summary of its purport in Greek. The translation of the inscription is, "To our lord, to Melkarth, lord of Tyre. The man offering is thy servant Obedasir and my brother. Both a son of Asirshamar, the son of Obedasir; when he hears their voice, may he bless them." On an inscription found in the ruins of Carthage, the name of this hero-divinity, according to the practice of the East, enters in composition into the names of individuals. Two have here the names of Obedmelearth and of Bedmelearth. According to Bochart, the town of Carteria was at first called Melcarteria, after this hero.† As an instance of the manner in which the events of this age were merged into the history of their deities, we may observe

* Justin, xliv., 4, 5. † "Canaan," lib. i., cap. 34.

that Cicero, who supposed the existence of six sacred persons with the name of Hercules, speaks of the Tyrian hero of that name as the son of Jupiter and Asteria, (*i. e.*, Baal and Ashtoreth,) and says that he had a daughter Carthago.*

This name was, as already observed, spelt by the Greeks in different ways, as Melkath, Melicertis, Miceris, and Midacritis. In the latter form it is found in Pliny, who, when giving a catalogue of worthies famous for useful discoveries and inventions, places this statement in the list: "Midacritus was the first who brought tin from the island called the Cassiteris." †

It remains for us to afford some further information respecting this traffic. From Gades there was a most extensive export trade in corn, wine, and oil of superior quality. Wax, honey, and pitch were also plentifully supplied for the foreign market; and, what was of inestimable value to a manufacturing people like the Phœnicians, the kermesberry, (*coccus tinctorius*,) used for making a scarlet dye, was found in large quantities. Stuffs of a very fine texture were manufactured in some

* *Natura Deorum*, lib. iii., 16.
† Pliny's "Natural History," lib. vii., 56.

parts of this country, and at first large quantities of woollen cloths were exported; but it was at length found more profitable to sell the wool, which was of very superior quality, in an unmanufactured state. The cattle were abundant and of a superior kind, and rams for breeding stock were sold at high prices. The fish produced along the coast are celebrated by Pliny as being exceedingly large and numerous. And as the country had some mineral salt and several saline springs, the curing and export of fish became a very extensive and profitable branch of commerce. But mining had a large share of attention, and the export of metals was a principal part of the outgoing trade of Gades. Not only Strabo, but Aristotle, Herodotus, and Pliny, speak of the immense metallic riches of the district of Tartessus at this period. Gold, silver, copper, lead, and iron were found in great abundance, and some small quantity of tin. These formed the staple of the Phœnician trade, and prepared them for prosecuting their commercial relations with the East, as they never could have done unless well supplied with the precious metals.

The neighbourhood of Gades was plentifully provided with timber well adapted for shipbuilding; so that here, as well as at Tyre, ships could be built or repaired with the greatest facility. This was an immense advantage to a people so devoted to commerce and navigation. Nor were these valuable products confined to the neighbourhood of Gades and Tartessus. "Of metals," says Strabo, "the whole country is full, although it is not equally fertile and flourishing throughout, especially in those parts where the metals most abound."* Among the Artabri, near Corunna, we are told that the earth is powdered with silver, tin, and gold, which are separated from the earth by being washed in sieves made like baskets.

We may now more particularly notice the trade with Britain, bearing in mind the assertion of Strabo, "that formerly the Phœnicians alone carried on this traffic from Gades."† According to him, the natives of Britain had tin, lead, and hides, which they bartered with the Phœnician merchants for earthenware, salt, and brasen vessels.‡ Dio-

* STRABO, lib. iii., cap. 8. † *Ibid.*, iii., v., 11.

‡ *Ibid.* The truth of this statement of has been doubted by the author of the excellent article, *Britannicæ Insulæ*, in Dr. W. Smith's "Dictionary of Geography," on the supposition that copper was raised and smelted in Britain, and that, consequently, bronze vessels could not be

dorus correctly states the locality of this commerce. "They," says he, "that inhabit the British promontory of Balerium,* by reason of their converse with strangers, are more civilized and courteous to strangers than the rest are. These are the people that prepare the tin, which, with a great deal of care and labour, they dig out of the ground; and that being rocky, the metal is mixed with some veins of earth, out of which they melt the metal, and then refine it; then they cast it into regular blocks, and carry it unto a certain island near at hand, called Ictis; for at low tide, all being dry between them and the island, tin in large quantities is brought over in carts."† As Balerium is the Land's End,

wanted. This assumption is, however, entirely gratuitous. No ancient author speaks of copper having been raised in Britain at this time. Even Pliny—who goes into detail, and gives the names of the principal places where this metal had been found, and of the persons who obtained celebrity by fusing and working it—says nothing of Britain in connexion with copper. (PLINY'S "Natural History," lib. vii., 57.) This metal is much more difficult to smelt than tin. It is well known that the Phœnicians worked copper mines in Cyprus and in other places; and the statement given in the text is confirmed by Cæsar, who asserts that the Britons imported brass. (*De Bello Gallico*, lib. v., c. xii.)

* The Land's End, Cornwall
† DIODORUS SICULUS, v., 2.

Diodorus does not describe the Cape itself, but the western part of the peninsula of Cornwall, which the imperfect geography of the Romans of that day believed to be a number of islands. Mr. Kenrick is perfectly correct in stating, that "the island, which at low water is joined to the mainland, can be no other than St. Michael's Mount,"* which was excellently adapted for the purpose of being a depôt for the trade between the foreign merchant and the miners on the mainland. It was also in the midst of the most productive tin mines of Cornwall. These are found near St. Just, and between it and Penzance, on one side; and Gwennap, Redruth, and Camborne, on the other: so that twelve miles to the west of St. Michael's Mount, and eighteen miles to the east of it, comprehend almost the whole of the ancient tin mining district.

We have already shown the improbability of the transfer of any British merchandise across the continent before the building of Marseilles and the location of the Belgæ in Britain. It becomes, therefore, desirable to ascertain as nearly as possible the date of the last-named event. This can only be done approximately. We know that their coming to Britain was

* "Phœnicia," p. 230.

subsequent to the settlement of the tribe in Gaul, and we have the means of fixing this date with tolerable accuracy. It will be shown that the Belgæ could not have been located in Britain much earlier than about B.C. 500. They were a German tribe who crossed the Rhine, and secured the possession of a large province in Gaul, directly opposite to Britain. The precise time of this irruption is not known; but we are told * that it was "of much later date" than the passage of a large band of Gauls into Germany under the command of Sigovesus. The history of this event states, that Ambigatrix, a king of the Gauls, finding the population of his country increase too fast for its resources, encouraged his two nephews to collect each of them a large body of people, and lead them forth to occupy other lands, as the gods might direct. Having made the necessary arrangements, Sigovesus, guided by the oracle, crossed the Rhine, and settled in the Hercynian Forest. Bellovesus, "at the head of an immense body of horse and foot," passed over the Alps, and occupied a portion of Italy.† Two historical facts enable us to ascertain, at least, very nearly the date

* "Ancient Universal History," vol. xvii., p. 29.
† Livy, book v., chap. 34.

of these emigrations. While Bellovesus was on his way to Italy, he found the Phocean Greeks, then recently arrived from Asia, struggling to establish themselves at Marseilles, and rendered them great assistance in fortifying the ground they had taken possession of on their landing; and when this Gallic chief arrived in Italy, Tarquinius Priscus was reigning at Rome. As it is well known that this Tarquin reigned from B.C. 618 to 578, and that Marseilles was founded about B.C. 600, it is clear that these irruptions into Germany and Italy must have taken place between B.C. 600 and 578. Then, as we are told that the Belgæ came into Gaul at "a much later date," that event could scarcely have occurred earlier than B.C. 550. It is also certain that they must have been a long time in Gaul before they would cross the channel, and obtain possession of the British coasts. This is rendered an undoubted fact by the statement of Cæsar, that the several tribes of the Belgæ on their settling in Britain called themselves by the names of the districts they had occupied in Gaul.* Of course this would only be done by a people who had resided a considerable time in those localities. Taking

* *Bel. Gal.*, v., 12.

all these circumstances into consideration, it does not seem probable that the Belgæ could have been settled in England earlier than the time named, B.C. 500.

The wide range of the maritime traffic of the Phœnicians is thus described by a living author :—" The colony of Gades outside the Strait formed the centre of a flourishing and extensive commerce, which reached on one side far to the south not less than thirty days' sail along the western coast of Africa,* and on the other side to Britain and the Scilly Islands. There were numerous Phœnician factories and small trading towns along the western coast of what is now the empire of Morocco; while the island of Kernê, twelve days' sail along the coast from the Strait of Gibraltar, formed an established depôt for Phœnician merchandise in trading with the interior. There were, moreover, towns not far distant from the coast, of Libyans or Ethiopians, to which the inhabitants of the central regions resorted, and where they brought their leopards' skins and elephants' teeth to be exchanged against the unguents of Tyre and the pottery of Athens. But this trade, though seemingly a valuable one, constituted only a small part of

* SALLUST. *Bel. Jug.*, c. 78.

the sources of wealth open to the Phœnicians of Gades. The Turditanians and Turduli, who occupied the south-western portion of Spain between the Arras river (Guadiana) and the Mediterranean, seem to have been the most civilized and improveable section of the Iberian tribes, well suited for commercial relations with the settlers who occupied the Isle of Leon, and who established the temple, afterwards so rich and frequented, of the Tyrian Hêraklês. And the extreme productiveness of the southern region of Spain in corn, fish, cattle, and wine, as well as in silver and iron, is a topic upon which we find but one language among ancient writers....For three or four centuries the Phœnicians had possessed the entire monopoly of this Tartesian trade, without any rivalry on the part of the Greeks: probably the metals there procured were in those days their most precious acquisition; and the tribes who occupied the mining regions of the interior found a new market and valuable demand for produce then obtained with a facility exaggerated into fable. It was from Gades, as a centre, that these enterprising traders, pushing their coasting voyages yet farther, established relations with the tin mines of Cornwall, perhaps also with the amber-gatherers from the coasts of the Baltic. It requires some effort to carry back our imaginations to the time when, along all this vast length of country, from Tyre and Sidon to the coast of Cornwall, there was no merchant ship to buy or sell goods, except these Phœnicians. The rudest tribes find advantage in such visitors; and we cannot doubt that the men whose resolute love of gain braved so many hazards and difficulties, must have been rewarded with profits on the largest scale of monopoly."*

Phœnicia is thus presented to our view in the early period of her commercial career as having all the Mediterranean maritime trade, an important traffic with the East through Egypt and Syria, and the whole of this Atlantic commerce; and these were held from thenceforward for several centuries. We are ill prepared to estimate the immense profits derived from these sources. In an instance which will be particularly specified hereafter, a Greek vessel destined for another port, with a cargo not selected with any view to the wants of Gades, by accident reached that harbour; and we are assured that the profit realized on that occasion was sixty talents, —equal to about sixteen thousand pounds

* Grote's "History of Greece," vol. iii., p. 370.

sterling.* If such was the gain on one chance shipment, what must have been the aggregate proceeds of this vast and long-continued traffic?

We need not be surprised, therefore, at the manner in which this commerce is spoken of by the sacred writers. Isaiah says of Sidon, "The harvest of the river is her revenue, and she is the mart of nations;" and speaks of Tyre as "the crowning city, whose merchants are princes, whose traffickers are the honourable of the earth."† And Ezekiel gives this glowing account of the commerce of Phœnicia, and of the wealth and glory with which it invested the metropolitan city: "Thy borders are in the midst of the seas, thy builders have perfected thy beauty. They have made all thy ship boards of fir-trees of Senir: they have taken cedars from Lebanon to make masts for thee. Of the oaks of Bashan have they made thine oars; the company of the Ashurites have made thy benches of ivory, brought out of the isles of Chittim. Fine linen with broidered work from Egypt was that which thou spreadest forth to be thy sail; blue and purple from the isles of Elishah was that

* Grote's "History of Greece," vol. iii., p. 376.
† Isaiah xxiii. 3–8.

which covered thee. The inhabitants of Zidon and Arvad were thy mariners: thy wise men, O Tyrus, that were in thee, were thy pilots. The ancients of Gebal and the wise men thereof were in thee thy calkers: all the ships of the sea with their mariners were in thee to occupy thy merchandise. They of Persia and of Lud and of Phut were in thine army, thy men of war: they hanged the shield and helmet in thee; they set forth thy comeliness. The men of Arvad with thine army were upon thy walls round about, and the Gammadims were in thy towers: they hanged their shields upon thy walls round about; they have made thy beauty perfect. Tarshish was thy merchant by reason of the multitude of all kind of riches; with silver, iron, tin, and lead, they traded in thy fairs. Javan, Tubal, and Meshech, they were thy merchants: they traded the persons of men and vessels of brass in thy market. They of the house of Togarmah traded in thy fairs with horses and horsemen and mules. The men of Dedan were thy merchants; many isles were the merchandise of thine hand: they brought thee for a present horns of ivory and ebony. Syria was thy merchant by reason of the multitude of the wares of thy making: they occupied in thy fairs with emeralds, purple, and broidered work, and fine linen, and coral, and agate. Judah, and the land of Israel, they were thy merchants: they traded in thy market wheat of Minnith, and Pannag, and honey, and oil, and balm. Damascus was thy merchant in the multitude of the wares of thy making, for the multitude of all riches; in the wine of Helbon, and white wool. Dan also and Javan going to and fro occupied in thy fairs: bright iron, cassia, and calamus, were in thy market. Dedan was thy merchant in precious cloths for chariots. Arabia, and all the princes of Kedar, they occupied with thee in lambs, and rams, and goats: in these were they thy merchants. The merchants of Sheba and Raamah, they were thy merchants: they occupied in thy fairs with chief of all spices, and with all precious stones, and gold. Haran, and Canneh, and Eden, the merchants of Sheba, Asshur, and Chilmad, were thy merchants. These were thy merchants in all sorts of things, in blue clothes, and broidered work, and in chests of rich apparel, bound with cords, and made of cedar, among thy merchandise. The ships of Tarshish did sing of thee in thy market: and thou wast replenished, and made very glorious in the midst of the seas."*

We have every reason for believing that this maritime ascendency of Phœnicia, and the flourishing state of her commerce, were continued with little or no interruption, until at least B.C. 500. But, prior to that period, the uninterrupted success of this people had produced its usual results, —rapine, injustice, and the outrage of the laws of humanity by unbridled violence. To what extent this was practised towards others we have no means of knowing; but, placed as they were in immediate contact with the Hebrews, we find in their sacred writings vivid descriptions of Phœnician cupidity and aggression on persons and property. Joel, who prophesied B.C. 800, bitterly complains on behalf of the Hebrews of Tyre and Sidon, and all the coasts of Palestina, "Because ye have taken away my silver and my gold, and have carried into your temples my goodly pleasant things: the children also of Judah and the children of Jerusalem have ye sold unto the Grecians."†
Amos, who ministered shortly afterwards, also denounced judgments on this people, because,

* Ezekiel xxvii. 4-25.   † Joel iii. 4-6.

in defiance of treaties subsisting between the two nations, they handed over whole bodies of captive Israelites to the Edomites, who were then great slave-dealers.* The "burden of Tyre," delivered by Isaiah, completes these prophetic maledictions, and is remarkable for the frequent allusion which it contains to Tarshish, as being involved in the same iniquity, and consequently threatened with a participation in the punishment impending over the mother country.†

In this prediction of Isaiah, the Chaldeans are mentioned as successors of the Assyrians, and from this people shortly afterwards Phœnicia was sorely assailed. The Hebrew tribes were at this time greatly weakened and humbled. The kingdom of Israel had suffered an irreparable loss in B.C. **747**, when Tiglath-pileser marched into Galilee, and the other northern parts of the kingdom, utterly subdued those districts, and carried the inhabitants into captivity.

Fearing Assyria on the one hand, and Egypt on the other, the rulers of Syria and Palestine were greatly terrified, and laboured to form alliances and combinations for their mutual protection. These efforts were para-

* Amos i. 9. † Isaiah xxiii.

lysed by the subjugation of this large portion of the kingdom of Israel: they were utterly defeated when the Assyrian sovereign, having received large gifts from Ahaz king of Judah, invaded Syria, slew Resin the king, spoiled Damascus the capital, took its citizens prisoners, and deported them to the East. Shalmaneser, who succeeded Tiglath-pileser on the throne of Assyria, was no less attentive to the extent of the Assyrian domination in the west of Asia than his predecessor. He invaded Samaria, weakened by the loss of its northern tribes, and after three years' siege subdued the city, and sent its inhabitants into Assyria. Not content with this success, he pushed on his aggression to the sea-coast, and invaded Phœnicia. We have in the "Antiquities" of Josephus a fragment preserved from Menander's History of Tyre, which refers to this precise period. It informs us that the Assyrian king, having invaded Phœnicia, detached many of the minor cities from their allegiance to Tyre, and induced them, as the sovereign city refused to submit to his authority, to unite their naval forces to attack it by sea. Tyre, we are told, was not backward in meeting this aggression. Collecting twenty-two vessels, the Tyrians attacked and completely defeated the opposing fleet, and captured five hundred prisoners. Perceiving that his design was frustrated, the Assyrian monarch retired, leaving a force sufficient to blockade Tyre on the land side, and to cut off its supplies of fresh water. Having perfect command of the sea, this measure still left the inhabitants quite at liberty. The lack of water they supplied by means of cisterns.*

While these unfavourable circumstances were transpiring in the East, an accident disturbed the quiet of the West. Psammetichus, king of Egypt, having abolished the restrictive policy of his predecessors by admitting the vessels of foreign nations to the entrance of the Nile, the Greeks, who were just entering on a career of maritime commerce, availed themselves of the opportunity, and freighted vessels to this new mart. One of these vessels, commanded by Colæus, and fitted out at Samos about B.C. 630, having a cargo intended for the Egyptian market, was, on its voyage towards Egypt, driven by a violent east wind far to the westward, until it found refuge for a while in the island of Platea. Believing, after some delay, that he should be

* Josephus, "Antiquities," ix., 14.

able to prosecute his voyage to Egypt, the commander left the island; but the winds continued to drive the vessel westward with great violence, until it was carried quite through the Straits, and, as if guided by more than human interposition, arrived at Tartessus. Here the cargo was sold to great advantage, so that, in gratitude for their deliverance, and for the large profit they had realized, the Samians provided a brasen vase, of the value of six talents, which was presented to the temple of Juno.*

There can be no doubt but that the success of this voyage, and the splendour of the votive offering, which Herodotus himself saw and admired, attracted great attention, and served as a stimulus to the rising maritime interest of Greece. But with this impulse, there also arose corresponding discouraging circumstances. By this time the Carthaginians had become a numerous and powerful people, treading in the steps of their fatherland, and maintaining a friendly relation with the parent state. This people most certainly participated largely in the trade with Gades and the other

---

* HERODOTUS, iv., 152. This is the voyage alluded to on page 119, which produced the extraordinary profits mentioned there. GROTE, vol. iii., p. 376.

ports in the Atlantic. But we have no means of marking the decadence of the parent, and the rising influence of the offspring, as all our authorities use the same terms when speaking of either of the two. The Carthaginians, therefore, sharing in the gains of this commerce, and inheriting the jealousy and exclusive views of the Tyrians, would undoubtedly be ready to use guile or force, to prevent any other nation entering upon what they regarded as their legitimate commercial domain.

The Greeks of Phocea were the most adventurous mariners whom that country had produced. Devoting themselves to navigation, they adapted their shipbuilding to the duties they had to perform, and the difficulties they had to encounter. Their vessels were not built as merchant vessels had previously been, round and capacious, adapted to carry the largest cargo, nor like the small war galleys of the Carthaginians; but were stout, well-armed vessels of fifty oars, each being capable of defending itself against any single opponent it was likely to meet. About B.C. 600, they founded the city of Massilia (Marseilles) at the mouth of the Rhone, and made that port a new centre for their western commerce. It appears that this city was built with the friendly acquiescence of some tribes of the Gauls in that neighbourhood; but having fully established themselves here, these adventurous Greeks sent out colonies, and founded Emporia and Rhodus, on the coast of Spain, in the Mediterranean. But previous to this period, the Phoceans had sailed to Gades, and had been received with so much favour by Arganthonius, king of Tartessus, that, on hearing of the continued aggressions which the Persians were making on their native country, he kindly invited them to abandon it, offering them permission to choose a place in his dominions in which to settle.* Although his offer was declined, this voyage, which took place about B.C. 570-560, opened a connexion between the Greeks and the grand mart of commerce in the West.

Soon after the building of Marseilles, the Persian general Harpagus assaulted Phocea with so much success, that, despairing of being able to oppose an adequate defence, the Phoceans embarked their families and goods on board their galleys, and sailed to Cyrnus, (Corsica,) where, about twenty years before, in one of their previous voyages to the West, they had founded a colony.† Here they re-

* Herodotus, i., 163.   Ibid., i., 165.

mained five years; but the settlement and operations of such energetic maritime merchants in the western Mediterranean roused the jealousy, and provoked the determined hostility, of those who had so long held the undisputed monopoly of these markets. The Carthaginians, aided, no doubt, by their Phœnician allies, fitted out a fleet, and proceeded with sixty vessels to attack the intruders. The Phoceans got together an equal number of ships, and a battle was fought, in which the Phoceans triumphed, though losing in the conflict nearly all their war vessels.*

These circumstances must have had an unfavourable influence on the trade of the West; but nothing contributed to this depressing effect so much as the new troubles which assailed Tyre. Nineveh having fallen before the combined forces of the Babylonians and Medes, and the Assyrian empire being thus terminated, Nebuchadnezzar assumed all the power it had exercised in Western Asia, and, having subdued the other cities of Phœnicia, began, B.C. 585, one of the most memorable sieges in history by investing Tyre. For thirteen years did the Babylonian monarch continue the struggle, and with equal per-

* HERODOTUS, i., 166.

severance did the determined Tyrians resist his power. Yet, although here, as in the former case, a fragment of Menander, preserved by Josephus, affords us important information, the result of the siege is still doubtful. That the Tyre which stood on the mainland was destroyed, is universally admitted; but it seems more than probable that in the meantime the island Tyre was greatly enlarged and extended, supported by the naval power which this people possessed, and thus the wealth and families of the Tyrians were saved from falling into the power of the proud Chaldean.*

Be this as it may, a siege like this, accompanied by such losses of life and property, as Tyre undoubtedly sustained, must, for a long time, have crippled its power, and rendered it

* It has been usually supposed that the insular Tyre was first built on this occasion. But from the information furnished by ancient authors, it is doubtful whether this was not the most ancient city. It was probably neglected after the erection of the city on the continent, and now on its ruin repaired, enlarged, and resorted to as the national metropolis. Even Sanchoniathon speaks of Astarte as consecrating worship "in the holy island of Tyre;" and it should also be remembered that it was the temple on insular Tyre to which the priests attributed such remarkable antiquity in their conversation with Herodotus. Jackson, having considered all the evidence, thinks the city on the island at least as old as Sidon. (" Chronological Antiquities," vol. iii., p. 30.)

unable to maintain its position against the rivals who were now becoming acquainted with the commerce of the Atlantic markets, and eager to grasp their share of its gains.

With the rise of the Persian power, and the progress of the arms of that empire in Western Asia, Phœnicia appears to have passed without resistance into the number of tributary states. But, notwithstanding all these reverses, as Phœnicia had still a widely extended commerce, means of wealth remained, which might have repaired the losses which had been suffered in the war with Babylon. Yet the trade with the East and with Egypt, although it yielded a most profitable revenue, not only hindered the Phœnicians from prosecuting new schemes of commercial discovery, but, in connexion with her altered political position, prevented her from retaining efficient control over her distant settlements. Notwithstanding that Carthage had always professed a filial relation to Tyre, it had been independent from the beginning; and now, if not earlier, Gades assumed a similar position.

During this period of Phœnician depression in the East, an impulse was given to the progress of geographical knowledge and commercial navigation in the West. Carthage fitted out two expeditions, under the command of two brothers. The precise date of this exploration is not known; but it has been placed at about B.C. 450. The first of these fleets was put under the command of Hanno, and was intended to explore the western coast of Africa, and to place a chain of settlements on its shores. It consisted of sixty ships, and carried no less than 30,000 colonists, including men, women, and children. Their object was accomplished, and six towns were raised, containing about 5,000 persons in each. The other expedition, under the charge of Hamilco, was intended to explore the western coast of Europe. This party also accomplished their intended object. They coasted the shores of Spain and Gaul, reached Britain, and found its tin market. The Periplus of Hanno, and the account of Hamilco's voyage, were both extant in ancient times, and were frequently referred to by writers of credit.* Both are now lost; but the certainty of Hanno's expedition is attested by an inscription fixed in one of the temples of Carthage, in which the principal events of this maritime exploration are detailed. The voyage of Hamilco is also certified to us

* PLINY, "Natural History," ii., 67.

by quotations from the account of it by Festus Avienus, in a poem, or metrical materials for a poem. (*Ora Maritima.*) Heeren has given us extracts which clearly indicate that the navigator reached the British islands. We copy one or two of the passages cited by Heeren. "Where the ocean flood presses in, and spreads wide the Mediterranean waters, lies the Alantic bay;* here stands Gadira, of old Tartessus; here the Pillars of Hercules, Abyla, left of Libya, and Calpe.†........Here rises the head of the promontory in olden times named Œstrymnon;‡ and below, the like-named bay and isles; wide they stretch, and are rich in metals, tin, and lead. There a numerous race of men dwell, endowed with spirit, and no slight industry, busied all in the cares of trade alone. They navigate the sea on their barks, built not of pines or oak, but, wondrous! made of skins and leather. Two days long is the voyage thence to the Holy Island, once so called, which lies expanded on the sea, the dwelling of the Hibernian race; at hand lies the isle of Albion. Of yore the trading voyages from Tartessus

* The bay between Cape St. Vincent and Cape Trafalgar.
† Here there is an omission.
‡ Probably Cape Finisterre.

reached to the Œstrymnides: but the Carthaginians and their colonies near the Pillars of Hercules, navigated in this sea, which Hamilco, by his own account, was upon during four months."* The "bay and isles rich in metals and tin" are St. Michael's Mount, Mount's Bay in Cornwall, and its neighbouring promontories, which might be taken for islands by a stranger. What settlements were planted by the Carthaginians on the shores thus explored, we do not know; but we find it asserted in the Periplus of Scylax, that "from the Pillars of Hercules on the European coast, there lay many settlements of the Carthaginians." We are not informed whether they made any establishments in Britain; but Heeren regards it as "placed beyond a doubt,"† that they visited the British Islands for commercial purposes.

About the same time as these voyages of Hanno and Hamilco were being made, another adventurous mariner appeared on the coast of Europe, prosecuting a series of observations and discovery. Pytheas was a native of Marseilles, a man of great courage and high

* *Ora Maritima*, quoted by HEEREN, "African Nations," vol. i., p. 503.

† HEEREN's "African Nations," vol. i., p. 101.

scientific acquirements, eminently qualified to promote the enlargement of commerce and the extension of geographical knowledge. The exact date of his voyage cannot be ascertained; but as his writings were well known in Greece in the time of Alexander the Great, his expedition can scarcely be placed later than B.C. 400. The statements of this writer have led to great differences of opinion. Among the ancients, Eratosthenes and Hipparchus refer to them as worthy of credit, while Polybius and Strabo denounce them as fabulous and false. A similar diversity of opinion exists among the eminent authors of the present day. Grote, in his "History of Greece," mentions him as a valuable author, and Sir G. C. Lewis speaks of him as altogether unworthy of belief. As this latter author has made Pytheas of so much importance in regard to the ancient navigation to Britain, it is necessary for us to allude more particularly to his case.

Grote says of him, "The loss of all details respecting the history of Massilia is greatly to be lamented; and hardly less, that of the writings of Pytheas, an intelligent Massiliotic navigator, who, at this early age, with an adventurous boldness even more than Phokœan, sailed through the Pillars of Hercules, and from thence northward along the coasts of Spain, Gaul, Britain, Germany; perhaps, yet further. Probably, no Greek, except a Massiliot, could have accomplished such a voyage; which in his case deserves the greater sympathy, as there was no other reward for the difficulties and dangers he had braved, except the gratification of an intelligent curiosity. It seems plain that the publication of his 'Survey of the Earth,' much consulted by Eratosthenes, though the criticisms which have reached us through Polybius and Strabo dwell chiefly upon its mistakes, real or supposed, made an epoch in geographical knowledge."*

Having mentioned this writer, Sir G. C. Lewis quotes the censures of Polybius and Strabo at large, and thus places before his readers a representation calculated to induce them to regard the production of the adventurous Massiliot with great distrust. We by no means intend to become his apologist. But when the works of an ancient author have perished, and he is only known to posterity by stray passages culled from his pages by unfriendly critics, we think he should not, on such evidence, be judged with great severity.

* Grote's "History of Greece," vol. xii., p. 620.

Polybius has laid down a rule for dealing with such authors, to which we heartily subscribe. Alluding to those who have " invented strange and incredible fictions of prodigies and monsters, reporting many things which they had never seen, and many also that had no existence," he says, " Since, therefore, all these circumstances concurred to render it not only difficult, but utterly impossible, to obtain any accurate and certain knowledge of those countries, we ought by no means to pass too severe a censure upon the old historians for their mistakes and omissions in these matters; but, on the contrary, should rather be persuaded, that they deserve our acknowledgments and thanks, on account even of the little information they have left behind them; and that, amid these numerous difficulties, they were able as it were to lay the foundation of more genuine discoveries."* If the excellent writer who laid down this rule, and some of his followers, had always observed it, they themselves would appear to greater advantage; and so would Pytheas.

We have here nothing to do with that perfect puzzle of all ancient geographers, that *terra incognita,* Thule; nor have we at present any

* POLYBIUS, book iii., chap. 5.

concern with the place whence amber was brought, whether from the Baltic, or elsewhere. But, looking simply at the exportation of tin from the south-west of the British island, we ask what the veracity or mendacity of Pytheas has to do with the question; seeing that it is supported by ample evidence from other sources. Sir G. C. Lewis does not deny the existence of Pytheas; he even admits that he sailed through the Straits of Hercules, and along part of the external coast of Europe.* This being the case, he may have been imposed on by those of whom he made inquiries, and may have committed serious errors in transmitting the hearsay information which he obtained; but it is certain, that he was in circumstances in which no intelligent person could fail to procure some knowledge of Britain and of the tin trade. Further, we may remark, that the inquiry naturally arises, If Strabo is a reliable authority when he censures Pytheas, why is he not an equal authority when he asserts, that "formerly the Phœnicians alone carried on this (tin) traffic from Gades" to the Cassiterides? If Polybius can be relied on when he corrects and censures the daring Massiliot, why is he not equally worthy of credit

* "Astronomy of the Ancients," p. 467.

when he speaks "of the British islands and their manner of making tin?"*

With regard to the observation, that ancient authors generally speak of Britain as unknown until the time of Cæsar, we feel placed in circumstances of great disadvantage. Alluding to the observation of Strabo, just quoted, that the Phœnicians made this voyage from Gades, "concealing the passage from every one;" a reviewer says, "This looks exactly like an hypothesis invented by the geographer, to account for a fact, the true cause of which was to him unknown." So when Scipio Africanus inquired of the people of Massilia, Narbo, and Corbilo on the Loire, and could get no information respecting Britain, it is inferred that the persons of whom he inquired could have known nothing of the country or its trade. It is scarcely possible to argue on a question of commercial policy with writers who, however learned, appear to have no conception that merchants have frequently some secrets connected with their business, and that, when they have, they know how to keep them.

The case of Cæsar is placed in the same category. And it is supposed, because he could get no information from the merchants

* POLYBIUS, book iii., chap. 5.

of Gaul respecting this island,* that they "knew scarcely anything in detail of Britain;" a conclusion completely disproved by the fact, that these merchants could instantly communicate the designs of Cæsar to the merchants on the other side of the channel. But we will assume that the inference is just, and that the Gallic merchants were as innocent and as ignorant as they are supposed to be; that they could neither inform Cæsar of the population of Britain, nor of their habits, or their harbours; and that all their knowledge related to the coast opposite Gaul. How are we to reconcile this with the alleged facts, that there was at that time an active tin trade going on, by which the great quantity of tin consumed by all the civilized states around the Mediterranean, and exported to Africa and the East, was brought from the extreme West of England to the Gallic ports opposite Britain, where it was landed and stored, and then sent across the whole country a journey of thirty days to Marseilles? and that this traffic had been going on for hundreds of years? If we would avoid falling into very serious error, we must not apply the commercial principles and laws at present in operation, to the case of the

* *Bel. Gal.*, iv., 20, 21.

ancients, whose circumstances differed from ours in almost every respect. In these days of newspapers and electric telegraphs, when information is disseminated with a rapidity and power that defies restraint, trade is open to universal competition. In the times of which we write, it was not so. Great success in commerce then mainly depended on the possession of some knowledge of goods, merchandise, or markets, which others did not possess; and when a merchant, or the merchants of any city or country, obtained such valuable information, it was guarded by them with the utmost care, and rendered subservient to important operations, and the acquisition of great wealth.

The voyage of Pytheas, whatever its extent, was unquestionably undertaken for the purpose of affording his countrymen such knowledge as would enable them to prosecute their commercial plans with greater advantage. How far this was effected we have no means of ascertaining; but it is an established truth, that Marseilles flourished as a rich and powerful commercial city, maintaining a first-rate rank as a maritime power, and sending out numerous colonies for extending her commercial interests.*

* STRABO, iv.; GROTE's "History of Greece," vol. xii., p. 613.

After Gades had become independent of Phœnicia, it is uncertain whether the other colonies followed her example in this respect. But in course of time all the colonies in the north of Africa, including Malta, were brought into subjection to the Punic power. This action clearly displays the striking contrast between the colonial policy of the parent state and that of Carthage. Phœnicia established her colonies with a view to commerce, and accordingly left them to govern themselves, satisfied with a monopoly of their trade as far as it could be secured. Carthage aimed at empire, and to this aim her important commercial policy became subordinate.

In these circumstances two centuries elapsed, during which we know very little concerning the operations at Gades. As there was a continual demand for the produce which the Atlantic emporia alone supplied, this commerce was continued; but the waning of the power of Persia, the brilliant era of Grecian arms and letters in the East, and the rising power of Rome and of Carthage in the West, fill up the history of these times.

The evident decline of Persia induced Egypt and Phœnicia, in the year B.C. 351, to throw off the yoke of her supremacy, and to assert their independence. But they had over-estimated their own power, or mistaken that of their former sovereign. They were soon brought again under subjection, Sidon being taken and destroyed in the struggle. This was only the prelude to a more terrible fate. In less than twenty years afterward, Alexander, having invaded Asia, laid siege to Tyre, and utterly destroyed it. But it is not improbable that it might have arisen again, phœnix-like, even from this ruin, if the conqueror had not reared up Alexandria in Egypt to take its place as the great emporium for the interchange of the merchandise of the East and the West. This measure consummated and perpetuated the ruin of Phœnicia.

It was probably soon after this event that the circumstances occurred which are recorded by Justin. Speaking of the removal of the sacred things of Hercules from Tyre to Gades, which would be likely to take place just prior to the entire destruction of the old city, he says, the neighbouring people of the country, being jealous of this city, attacked "the Gaditani in war." This assault was so powerful, that Gades was obliged to seek aid from Carthage; which, we are told, was promptly and efficiently supplied. "The expedition being successful, they both secured the Gaditani from injury, and added the greatest part of the province to their own dominions." *

From henceforth the commerce of Gades, and the other marts on the shores of the Atlantic, must be regarded as thrown open to considerable competition. From the conduct of the king of Tartessus to the Phocean voyagers long before this time, it is very plain that the natives of that territory had learned the value of the productions of their country, and had asserted their right to participate in the trade which had been created. Carthage, by the assistance which it had rendered to Gades, and the success of her arms in the neighbourhood, had adopted means for extending her influence on the Spanish soil, and sharing more largely than heretofore in the profits of the commerce of Western Europe. For some considerable period this purpose was certainly secured. By means of her influence at Gades and her colonies in Spain, every opportunity was afforded to Carthage to grasp a dominant power over the Spanish and British trade. But her aims at empire here again interfered with her commercial interests. The building of Carthagena, and the attempt to

* JUSTIN, xliv., 5.

add Spain to her dominions, brought her once more into fatal conflict with Rome, from whom she had already suffered much. Eighty years of alternate bloody war and deceitful peace, from the foundation of the Punic city on the east coast of Spain, sufficed to blot the name of Carthage for ever from the roll of independent nations, and to place her soil among the number of Roman provinces.

During this period Massilia luxuriated in the highest commercial prosperity. This merchant city neither devoted her own people to any great extent to the profession of arms, nor, like other great centres of trade, relied for her home protection on mercenary troops. Situated very near to Rome, who in her martial pride had proscribed commerce on her own soil,* Massilia mainly depended on her connexion with the imperial city for defence in any emergency. And the position of the Greek community was such, that for a long season its friendship amply repaid Rome for the protection which the rising commercial city received. Thus, " under the shelter of this great military power, their commerce flourished and expanded on all sides. Syracuse and Carthage were crushed by the uni-

* Merivale's "Roman Republic," p. 8.

versal conqueror; the maritime power of the Etrurians had already dwindled away before they fell under his baneful domination. The mercantile genius of Greece, which had migrated from Athens to Rhodes and Corinth, was impaired by internal weakness, and repressed by the harassing activity of the pirates in the Eastern Mediterranean. Accordingly *Massilia reigned for a considerable period without a rival in the career of commerce.* But her trade was mainly supplied by the produce and the wants of the vast continent which lay behind her." * If the mineral produce of the western parts of Britain was ever landed in Gaul, and carried across that country to Massilia, it must have been during the period in which that city enjoyed this commercial ascendancy.

It is, however, very unlikely that this could have been done, until the imperial power had fully reduced Gaul into the condition of a Roman province. Notwithstanding all the support which Massilia received from her Roman ally, Mr. Merivale freely admits, that "it with difficulty maintained its own existence against the tribes of the interior." † Is

---

* Merivale's "History of the Romans under the Empire," vol. i., p. 229.

† *Ibid.*, p. 228.

it probable that in those circumstances a regular succession of valuable merchandise could be carried across the Continent from the Atlantic to the mouth of the Rhone? That this was subsequently done there is little doubt. As the author already quoted has observed, " Massilia opened regular communications with the interior of Gaul, and from thence with the ocean and the British isles; thus substituting a direct and safer route for the perilous circumnavigation of the Phœnician coasting vessels." *

This might of course be expected, as soon as the land route was more direct and more safe than the transit by sea. But before that time, to a people like the Massiliots, who had no military posts in the interior, who had frequently to maintain war with the tribes occupying the neighbouring districts even for their existence, and who were also possessed of the best mercantile marine then in the world, the land route could not be more safe than the sea voyage.

But when the campaigns of Cæsar had completely reduced Gaul to subjection under the imperial power, and Massilia was brought under the Roman government, then the land

* " History of the Romans under the Empire," vol. i., p. 229.

transit would become feasible, and was unquestionably adopted.

This conclusion agrees with the history of the times and the authorities we have quoted. Cæsar subdued the last effort of Gallic independence about B.C. 50, after which date the Roman domination proceeded to harmonize discordant elements, and to blend the nations of Western Europe into friendly concert for their mutual advantage. In B.C. 30, Augustus obtained supreme dominion over the Imperial State, and gave peace to the world: this was proclaimed the following year by the shutting of the temple of Janus. These events afforded unrestricted action to commerce. Merchants could then adopt the best means for conducting their business, and the best modes of transit for the conveyance of their goods. After this state of things had existed twenty years, Diodorus wrote, that the British tin was taken from Ietis to the coast of France, and thence across the country to the mouths of the Rhone. No one can reasonably doubt the truth of this statement: it is sanctioned by every probability, and all the dictates of common sense. But that this was the route pursued a thousand years before, is in our judgment an impossibility.

After a candid and careful inquiry into the whole subject, our conclusion is, that between B.C. 1500 and B.C. 1200 the Phœnicians sailed into the Atlantic, discovered the mineral fields of Spain and of Britain, and enjoyed a monopoly of this commerce for several centuries, trading directly with both countries: That afterwards, as the power of successive nations rose and waned, this traffic was shared by the Greeks, Carthaginians, Gaditani, Massiliots, and others; and when the world was subjected to the sway of Rome, the general course of the tin trade was that indicated by Diodorus, namely, from Ictis to the French coast, and thence overland to Marseilles.

In compiling our summary of information respecting this ancient commerce, we have no expectation of securing universal assent to our conclusions. We have, however, to the best of our ability, with the limited time and means at our command, redeemed our pledge, and given a brief but complete investigation of the subject. We have done this under a conviction that it is not only worthy of careful research, but demands it, and ought to be canvassed until the truth attainable respecting it has been elicited and exhibited to the public. We recall attention to the simple fact, that tin was an article of ancient commerce, at least as early as B.C. 1200, on the eastern shores of the Mediterranean. This is an established truth. Notwithstanding all the speculations which Beckmann has so laboriously conceived and collected,* it is certain that tin was used and sold at Sidon and Tyre at this early date. No historical evidence can be adduced to prove that it was brought from the East. Whence then did it come? The universal testimony of all history and tradition answers, From Britain. This testimony has been received, and the British origin of the tin supplied as an article of commerce in the earliest times has been believed, by great numbers of learned men in different ages and countries. Having carefully studied the subject, they have been fully convinced that the ancient Phœnicians traded with Britain for this metal, and regularly took it from the coast of this island in Phœnician ships to Tyre and

* "Bronze, which is one of the oldest alloys of copper we are acquainted with, contains about ten or twelve per cent. of tin." It has been found by analysis that this is just the composition of the bronze instruments found in the sepulchral barrows of Europe, of the nails which fastened the plates to the roof of the treasury of Atreus, at Mycenæ, and of the instruments found in the tombs of ancient Egypt. (KENRICK's "Phœnicia," p. 213.)

Sidon. The names of those who have entertained this opinion would, if collected, exhibit a body as numerous, as intelligent, and as entitled to deference and respect, as could be found supporting almost any historical truth.

There are men, however, who dissent from this judgment, some of whom deny that tin in these early ages came from Britain. Others object that Phœnician ships fetched it from thence, but maintain that, if obtained from this island, it was carried across the Continent to the mouths of the Rhone. We have assigned reasons for the opinions we have formed, and we think this should be done by those who take conflicting views. If it is maintained that tin was not brought from Britain, we respectfully ask, Whence was it brought? If Phœnician ships did not then visit our shores for the purchase of tin, what maritime people did? Was the metal taken a thousand years before our era from Cornwall to the coast of France in British coracles, made of osiers and skins, or by what other means? How was this commodity transferred to the mouths of the Rhone hundreds of years before Marseilles and Narbo were built?

We propound these questions with great

respect and seriousness. We will venture to say that we have stated a means by which this market, in the earliest ages, might have been supplied. That the Phœnicians traded to Gades is an undoubted fact; and, this being admitted, the possibility of their reaching Cornwall cannot be denied. If, then, this is deemed improbable and incredible, let us have some probable and credible means exhibited, by which the metal was taken to the East. We repeat that this ought to be done. When men who have established a world-wide reputation for learning, and those who conduct periodicals which are circulated over the globe, repudiate what has been long and widely held as an undoubted truth, we have a right to ask for a substitute to fill up the chasm and restore unity and completeness to our knowledge of the subject. In a case like this, when the old popular tradition of Phœnician intercourse with Britain is denied, the world is entitled to something more from such quarters than an uninstructive expression of scepticism,—a barren declaration of disbelief. The world has outlived the day when the *dictum* of the learned could create or annihilate an article of popular faith. It is now happily essential that facts and reasons be given, if old errors are to be exploded, or new truths fixed in the public mind. When this is done, we shall be ready with frankness and candour to correct our judgment on this subject; but till then, no mere expressions of doubt or disbelief, however high the source whence they emanate, will shake our faith in "conclusions" which we believe to be founded on legitimate historical evidence, and worthy to be regarded as established truths.

www.ingramcontent.com/pod-product-compliance
Lightning Source LLC
Chambersburg PA
CBHW030301170426
43202CB00009B/829